Safe To Breathe?

Safe To Breathe?

David Farmer
BA LLB FInstPet MIOSH

John Humphrey
BSc CEng MIChemE FIOSH FIRM

Croner Publications Ltd
Croner House
London Road
Kingston upon Thames
Surrey KT2 6SR
Tel: 01-547 3333

Copyright © 1989 Kingwood
This edition first published 1989

Published by
Croner Publications Ltd,
Croner House,
London Road,
Kingston upon Thames,
Surrey KT2 6SR
Telephone 01-547 3333

While every care has been taken
in the writing and editing of this book,
readers should be aware that only Acts of Parliament
and Statutory Instruments have the force of law,
and that only the courts can authoritatively
interpret the law.

British Library Cataloguing in Publication Data

Farmer, David, 1928 –
Safe to breathe? 2nd ed. – Croner health and
safety guides)
1. Great Britain. Workplaces. Air. Pollution Safety Levels.
Legal aspects
I. Title
344.104'46342

ISBN 1-85452-013-X

Contents

Introduction

It is not a new idea to have nationally published figures indicating when the concentration of an airborne gas, vapour or dust in a workplace is approaching a level dangerous to workers' health.

In 1984 occupational exposure limits, called Control Limits and Recommended Limits, were accorded a new status by the Health and Safety Commission.

On 1.10.89 these limits will change in name and status again, and Maximum Exposure Limits (MELs) and Occupational Exposure Standards (OESs), introduced by the Control of Substances Hazardous to Health Regulations 1988 (COSHH), will become an integral part of the regime controlling health in the workplace.

This book gives the background to the present and former regimes, describes how the new limits are to be operated and comments on their legal significance. It also deals with the practical aspects of identifying and measuring the contaminants, and the establishment and maintenance of an effective management system for monitoring performance, so that concentrations are kept at levels "so far as reasonably practicable" below the point at which they are capable of inflicting harm.

Chapter 1

Risks to health at work

Airborne hazardous substances at work overcome the body's natural defences and cause temporary or permanent harm. The harmful effects vary in the time they take to appear; whether they are direct or indirect; and which parts of the body they affect.

Hazardous substances can be inhaled, absorbed through broken or unbroken skin, come into contact with the skin or eyes, or be ingested (taken into the gut). They are either non-particulate gases or vapours, particulate dusts or fibres, micro-organisms or airborne droplets of liquid.

Good Health

When we feel on top of the world and our bodies are functioning normally, we describe the phenomenon, together with the sense of mental well-being that usually goes with it, as good health. Body and mind are in tune; the senses respond naturally to all the normal stimuli; we experience what is going on around us unimpeded by pain, discomfort, anxiety or disease.

To maintain the human body in this state we must take in food, drink and air. The body absorbs what it needs from them and excretes the unwanted remainder.

Body's defences

Along with the substances vital to continued healthy existence and growth, other substances are taken into the body which are harmful to it in varying degrees. The body is not, however, totally vulnerable to these unwanted and harmful materials. It possesses its own defence mechanisms. For example, the hairs in the nose serve as a primary dust filter, tears bathe the eyeball and the liver and kidneys are quite efficient organs of detoxification (extracting toxic materials and excreting them via bile, faeces and urine).

With such defence mechanisms, which usually work away unnoticed, there comes a time when, if called upon to cope with harmful materials in quantity or for too long, the defences become overwhelmed and break down. This may be wholly or in part, either temporarily or permanently.

Many of the harmful materials are encountered at the workplace and are absorbed into the bodies of those exposed to them there. Most countries therefore have worker protection laws which recognise this fact and seek in them to impose duties on employers to take positive steps to stop their workers from becoming ill. The United Kingdom recently enacted far-reaching new regulations to tackle all occupational health problems except those few already subject to their own separate regulations (ie lead, asbestos, radiation and hazardous substances encountered below ground in mines).

Substances administered to a person in the course of medical treatment are excepted, as are substances hazardous to health solely by virtue of their explosive or flammable properties or solely because they are at a high or low temperature or high pressure.

The full title of the regulations is The Control of Substances Hazardous to Health Regulations 1988 but they are almost always referred to now simply as the COSHH regulations. COSHH does not, however, displace existing public health and environmental health law, such as the Public Health Acts and Food Hygiene (General) Regulations 1970.

To frame such laws and to understand how they can work and how they can be enforced, it is necessary to know something about the way toxic materials enter the body and what happens when they get there. It is necessary to understand enough physiology and toxicology to appreciate the link between the hazard and the measures required to eliminate it, or reduce it to an acceptable level. This assumes that an acceptable level exists at all. Part of COSHH (regulation 12) is aimed specifically at those who are at risk from exposure to toxic materials. It intends that they should be provided with such information, instruction and training to tell them all they need to know about the hazardous substances they work with and the precautions which should be adopted when using them to avoid suffering from any acute or chronic ill-effects.

The information needs to cover the nature and degree of the risks to people's health and any factors, such as smoking, which could increase those risks. It also needs to include a full understanding of how the control measures work. The nature of the control measures, how they are maintained and how any defects in them can be spotted early (eg: tell-tale piles of dust adjacent to ventilation ducting, or pools of liquid near to pipe flanges) are all important subjects to be included in the operator's general workplace health education. Without such knowledge employees are unable to exercise the reasonable care which it is their statutory duty to fulfil under the provisions of the Health and Safety at Work, etc Act 1974.

Exercising reasonable care is not instinctive: it has to be based upon clearly understood facts about the substances concerned.

Harmful effects

There are a number of ways of looking at the harmful effects brought about by toxic substances encountered at the workplace.

Firstly, there is the *type of effect* which can be brought about. This can vary from the insidious but not unpleasant feeling of drowsiness experienced in the early stages of, often fatal, carbon monoxide poisoning, to the tearful and choking distress wrought by ammonia or chlorine fumes in quite low concentrations. Again, a toxic vapour could affect the central nervous system and lead to blinding headaches or affect the digestive system and lead to griping colic. It is only in the case of fumes like ammonia or chlorine that there is an unequivocal connection between the symptoms and the exposure. In many instances of occupational illness and disease the connection is not always detected because it is not always obvious. This is one of the principal difficulties of the subject.

Secondly, there is the *time-scale of the effect,* which can vary from seconds to years. Some toxic materials are immediately harmful and bring about acute effects within a very short time of the first instant of exposure. Other toxic materials accumulate slowly within the body until their presence eventually interferes with normal bodily functions. The chronic pneumoconiosis sufferer is a prime example of the long-term toxic effects of exposure to dust.

Thirdly, there is the *site of the effect*. Some substances affect the skin; others the lungs; some the blood or the liver; some the eyes; and so on.

Toxic materials in the body inflict different kinds and degrees of damage on different organs as they pass through them. Some solvents, for example, inflict long-term internal damage on the liver and also cause in those handling them, short term degreasing of the skin, frequently accompanied by soreness, cracking, infection and dermatitis.

Finally, there is the *type of agent* which causes harm. It is sufficient here to say that this book is mainly concerned with harm brought about by atmospheric contamination because inhalation of airborne contaminants is the most frequent method of entry into the body. However, studies undertaken since 1984, when the first edition was published, suggest that it would be wrong to underestimate the role of the skin as an entry route into the body by hazardous materials. Research by Australian scientists, for example, is casting doubts on the long-held belief that lead can not be absorbed through the skin in significant amounts. "Lead-in-sweat" levels measured as part of the studies suggest this is not the case and that lead can be absorbed through the skin quite quickly in significant and undesirable amounts. In the United Kingdom the Health and Safety Executive is also embarking upon research to seek out further information on the same subject. The primary objective of the research is to develop a strategy for monitoring and controlling the absorption of hazardous substances through the skin. Referring to its own proposed research, the Health and Safety Executive's Toxic Substances Bulletin (December 1988) states that a wide range of substances, including pesticides, pharmaceuticals and other industrial chemicals, as well as solvents, is well known to penetrate the skin, but the "importance of skin absorption in the development of systemic toxicity is not yet clear *and may have been underestimated*".

Type of toxic effect

The extent and nature of the damage caused by toxic materials varies enormously. Here it is not possible to attempt any systematic description of what all the different types of materials do to the body, but just to illustrate some of the more common damaging effects.

Direct physical damage

Certain substances assault the body directly. The graphic international symbol for corrosive substances speaks for itself. It shows the flesh of a hand being eaten away. Into this category come many acids, alkalis, halogens and their salts, organic halides, organic acid halides, esters and their salts and a miscellaneous group of chemicals including hydrazine and silver nitrate.

Indirect damage

In one sense the very nature of the harm described above carries with it its own warning. As with molten metal the hazard is almost always immediately and compellingly obvious. Unfortunately many materials classed as toxic do not work in such a direct way. They are absorbed by the body in one of the ways described below and damage or inhibit the function of one or more internal organs. The liver, for example, has its effectiveness as an organ impaired when it has to deal with solvents over an extended period. This impairment is brought about by the metabolism of the solvents in the liver and the production of compounds there which kill liver cells and lessen the organ's ability to work as it should.

Another example of indirect damage is that caused by the gradual accumulation of dust particles which elude the normal scavenging mechanisms operated by the lungs. The damage is indirect in the sense that the presence of the dust in quantity and the fibrosis or scarring caused by it, do not allow the oxygen/carbon dioxide interchange which the lungs normally perform, to take place as efficiently as it should, Other ill effects follow from the deterioration.

Sometimes a substance inhibits the body's normal biochemical pattern resulting in ill-health. A good example of such inhibitory effects is that brought about by exposure to organophosphorus pesticides following their absorption, normally through the skin. The toxic effects arise, especially in the blood and nervous system, because of the inhibition of the cholinesterase group of enzymes.

A final example of an indirect effect is that created by TDI (toluene di-isocyanate) used in the manufacture of polyurethane plastics. Breathing in TDI affects the body's immune system and causes it to go wrong. It sets up an allergic reaction and gives rise to a sensitisation in the victim. This in turn is capable of being triggered off thereafter by very short exposure to minuscule amounts of TDI and establishes a distressing asthmalike condition in the victim.

Before leaving the subject of indirect damage there has to be a reference to the emotive topic of the genetic and carcinogenic effects which certain substances encountered in industry are known to have. Much is now known about the subject but there still remains a very great deal more to learn. It is sufficient for the purpose of this book to state that because of the frequently fatal prognosis in cancer cases, however the condition is brought about, the most stringent controls are imposed by regulatory bodies. In some instances the use of certain substances is prohibited. Substances subject to prohibition are to be found in schedule 2 of COSHH reproduced on page 84.

Time-scale of toxic effect

It has been said that in industry the quickest way to ill-health is by an explosion where, milliseconds after detonation, traumatic injuries (burns and injuries caused by flying debris entrained in the blast) are inflicted on those in the vicinity. This book is not concerned at all with these types of industrial incidents, or the traumatic, instant mayhem which can result from them. However, it is concerned with effects which are acute and follow almost immediately after exposure to a toxic substance. The example of TDI was given in the last section where a very short exposure can give rise to symptoms quite quickly. Another toxic substance capable of bringing about very sudden effects is hydrogen sulphide. In high concentrations paralysis of the respiratory centre can cause sudden unconsciousness, asphyxia and death. One characteristic which is particularly unfortunate with this substance, renowned for its strong smell of rotten eggs, is that it very rapidly deadens the sense of smell. The potentially lethal consequences to anyone not fully aware of this effect on encountering the gas, can easily be imagined.

In the case of exposure to nickel carbonyl, to take another example, its highly insoluble vapour penetrates the lungs and results in an abnormal accumulation of fluid termed oedema. This effect and the difficulty with breathing appear after about two days. The period between exposure and the appearance of the symptoms is referred to as the latent period.

In the case of some toxic effects the latent period can be as long as forty years eg: asbestosis/lung cancer. Herein lies another of the main dilemmas of occupational medicine. Many workers may today be working in environments contaminated by materials not currently classed as toxic but which may be found to be so at some time in the future.

Similarly, there are workers severely affected by crippling illness today attributable to their past workplace exposure to substances which, at the time of that exposure, were not recognised as harmful at all, or not as harmful as they later were discovered to be.

A good example of a substance not originally recognised as being very harmful but which we now know to be lethal, is asbestos. A Home Office survey of the asbestos industry in 1910-1911 did not disclose "any evidence of the existence of a serious health hazard in the industry". By 1928 a case of "non-tubercular fibrosis of the lungs in an asbestos worker of sufficient severity to necessitate treatment in hospital" prompted an investigation. As a result of the enquiry the future of the industry was still regarded optimistically. It was believed that "the effect of the energetic application of preventive measures should be apparent in a great reduction in the incidence of fibrosis". By 1931 regulations had been made. Later in the 1930s about 40% of men with asbestosis were recorded as dying of lung cancer. By 1963 the percentage had passed the 50% mark. The strong synergistic link between cigarette smoking and cancer of the lung had also become firmly established by this time. In the 1960s a further link between asbestos and mesothelioma, an invariably fatal malignant tumour of the pleura and peritoneum, was also established.

In the space of four decades a substance first regarded as a nuisance dust changed to one known to be a lethal carcinogen. The cautionary tale of asbestos is a salutary one underlining, above all, the importance of recognising the possible length of the latent period between the start of exposure to a substance and the onset of symptoms from which there is little or no relief.

The problem of latency also has another practical drawback concerned with the establishment and maintenance of awareness among the exposed working population. The longer the time between exposure and visible obvious symptoms, the harder it is to convince workpeople of the nature of the risk and of the need to adopt precautions. Nowhere is this more manifest than in the case of occupationally-induced deafness. This condition, although outside the direct scope of this book, illustrates very well the sad fact that usually by the time a deteriorating bodily function is noticed by the individual concerned, the process is irreversible and prospects for recovery are either limited or non-existent. This is certainly true of noise-induced hearing loss (NIHL), which is dealt with more fully in "Too Loud?" published by Croner Publications.

Site of effect

Some chemicals have an affinity for certain organs but this does not mean that it is necessarily those organs which also sustain the most damaging effects. Lead has an affinity for the bones but lead is not toxic to them. The symptoms of lead poisoning come from the presence and effects of lead in the soft tissues.

Consideration of the all-important subject of the route of entry of toxic materials into the body is deferred until later. It is sufficient to emphasise here the subject's complexity. The site of the immediate effect may be, for example, the eyes where profuse watering occurs. The lungs and airways may then be similarly irritated as the gas is breathed in. The gas then becomes dissolved in the blood and transported to other organs where further damage may be sustained before excretion finally occurs or the toxic material lodges in some particular organ for which it has an affinity (eg: certain kinds of pesticides in the body fat; benzene in the bone marrow).

Route of harmful agents into the body

(a) **Inhalation**
Obviously the form of a harmful agent governs very much the route by which it can enter and be absorbed into the body of those exposed to it. Unless a toxic solid is broken down into fragments small enough to become airborne it can not be inhaled (taken into the lungs by breathing in). Similarly, unless a liquid passes into a gaseous state it can not be breathed in, only swallowed or splashed onto the skin. *Inhalation is by far the commonest route of entry of toxic substances into the body.*

(b) **Skin absorption**
Percutaneous or skin absorption is a second but less

common route of entry. It occurs when the substance is absorbed through the intact skin, either via the cells of the skin itself, or via the hair follicle, sebaceous, or sweat gland openings. Because it is less common as an entry route it is all the more important to be aware of it. The tables of occupational exposure limits published annually by the Health and Safety Executive (Guidance Note EH40) indicate where it is known that substances can be absorbed through the skin.

While solvents and other chemical substances such as phenol and aniline can penetrate the unbroken skin, hazardous substances such as micro-organisms can easily enter the body via cuts, scratches and abrasions. A good example of this is leptospirosis (Weil's disease). This is caused by a bacteria contracted by contact with infected urine, most commonly of rats, and encountered by miners, sewer workers, farmworkers, abattoir workers, etc. Otherwise, the unbroken skin is protected to some extent by the sweat glands and sebum (a waxy substance secreted by sebaceous glands) acting both as a physical and chemical barrier effective against many micro-organisms.

It must not be supposed that a toxic substance may only enter the body by one route. As already indicated the vapour from a substance may be inhaled and liquid droplets near the surface of a vessel may splash onto the uncovered hands and arms and be absorbed through the skin.

(c) **Ingestion**

The third route of entry of toxic or harmful materials is through the gastro-intestinal tract or gut. Absorption of toxic material through the gut is called ingestion. Whereas ingestion is a common route in the non-occupational sphere (eg: drug overdose, food poisoning, accidental swallowing) it is the least common direct entry route for those at work. It may however be an indirect entry route in the following way. Airborne material, small enough to penetrate the lungs may impact onto the film of mucous lining the lung tissue and then be raised by an escalatory movement out of the airways into the throat from whence it transfers to the stomach and digestive tract.

This introductory chapter concludes by describing the

form of airborne contaminants. It has to be appreciated that form has a major influence on how and how much of the material becomes absorbed by the body and hence is capable of wreaking its harmful effect.

Substances breathed into the lungs are either particulate or non-particulate. The air which we breathe is a mixture of both. It is a mixture of the non-particulate oxygen, nitrogen and carbon dioxide and traces of a number of other gases, together with the tiny particulate fragments of organic and inorganic material which have become airborne. Only the smaller particles remain airborne for long in air. The heavier ones fall by gravity and lie where they fall. Some of the smallest particles can remain almost permanently airborne, however, because constant turbulence in the air creates a force greater than that of the force of gravity, tending to make the particles fall and settle. Sometimes the smallest particles are visible with the naked eye only when caught in a ray of sunlight.

A dust observation method using the "ray-of-sunlight" technique was pioneered by John Tyndall whose Tyndall beam apparatus enables otherwise invisible dust to be seen and its behaviour studied. The observation method and the apparatus used is commented on further in Chapter 4.

As an instructional tool it is invaluable. Not only is this so for the occupational hygienist making a preliminary dust survey but it can be invaluable to convince those workers exposed to dust they can not see, that it is there in quantities which over a period of time may have a life-shortening effect on them. After such a demonstration, it becomes easier to relate their work patterns to good working practices which minimise the evolution of dust. It also enables those instructing them to overcome the initial barrier of disbelief.

"What the eye cannot see, the heart cannot grieve over" sums up a very natural reaction to being told that dust which cannot be seen with the naked eye can be the cause of lung disease many years hence. The Tyndall beam at least overcomes part of the challenge: it shows that the dust is there and that the pathways it follows are often in the worker's breathing zone.

Form of harmful agents

Non-particulates

(a) *Gases and vapours*

Gases and vapours are usually dealt with together. The term "gas" is applied to any material in the gaseous state at normal temperature and pressure (ie: 25°C and 760mm Hg)

The term "vapour" is applied to the gaseous phase of a substance which is ordinarily a liquid or solid at normal temperature and pressure. Some confusion about the two terms exists not only because the United Kingdom Factories Act 1961 definition of fume includes gas or vapour but because the word fume is often loosely applied to *any* airborne contaminant. It should be used only as detailed below. What the lung receives in gaseous form is transferred by diffusion from its air sacs to the capillary blood and thence it circulates in the blood through the rest of the body and may affect other organs en route.

Particulates

Aerosols
Technically, the word aerosol should only be applied to describe a dispersion of solid or liquid particles in a gas. It has, however, passed into more common use to describe pressurised airspray cans used for dispensing such domestic products as paint, hair lacquer, or insecticides. The toxicologically significant classes of aerosol are named and defined below.

(a) *Dusts*

Aerosols consisting of inorganic or organic solid material are called dusts and vary widely in particle shape and size. Dusts are formed by mechanical disintegration of a parent material by grinding, sanding, sawing, drilling, handling or transporting. If the particle shape is roughly spherical we call the dust compact (eg: coal dust), otherwise it is termed fibrous (eg: asbestos, cotton). The significance of the shape lies in the influence it has in determining particle behaviour and destination in the body. Particle shape and size are quite critical factors.

(b) *Fumes*

Fumes are collections of particles suspended in a gas (usually air) the size of each of which is below 0.1 micrometre. Their formation by combustion, sublimation or condensation is usually accompanied by a chemical change such as oxidation. The commonest fumes of significance toxicologically are those associated with oxides of metals.

(c) *Smokes*

Smokes are collections of particles which are below 0.5 micrometres in size. Smokes are formed during the combustion of organic materials and arise from incomplete combustion.

(d) *Mists and fogs*

Mists and fogs are liquid droplets formed by the condensation of vapours or the atomisation of liquids around particulate nuclei in air, or by the uptake of liquid by hygroscopic (ie: absorbent) particles.

Conclusions

If the health of workers is to be maintained it is vital that those harmful substances capable of undermining it are identified, recognised and efficiently controlled. This implies both legal and practical control.

In the case of the former it is relatively simple to achieve it in the extreme case by the imposition of an outright ban upon the use of a particularly hazardous substance. This has been a method adopted sparingly but it has been used with certain carcinogens as mentioned earlier. A less dramatic method which has been in use for some years in a number of countries is the establishment of exposure limits. Over the years different descriptions have been applied to the limits in different parts of the world. The terms Maximum Permissible Limits (MPLs); Maximum Acceptable Concentrations (MACs); Threshold Limit Values (TVLs); Maximum Permissible Concentrations (MPCs); Maximale Arbeitsplatzkonzentration (MAKs); Valori Limite

Ponderati (VLPs), have all been used and whilst they are all concerned with putting a numerical value to a concentration believed to mark roughly the borderline between relative safety and increasing danger, there are differences in their methods of derivation, adoption, legal status and role in enforcement. The idea behind them all is the same. The use of exposure limits in this country, their terminology, role and legal status are all matters dealt with in the next two chapters.

Chapter 2

Legal Duties

Drawing precise lines for limiting atmospheric contamination is legally and technically quite difficult, taking into account differing individual susceptibilities, synergism and persisting uncertainty about the toxicological effects of many substances. The American Threshold Limit Values (TVL) system was followed from the 1970s using time-weighted averages, short term exposure limits and ceiling limits.

These were replaced in 1984 by Occupational Exposure Limits (OELs) which were either called Control Limits or Recommended Limits.

These have been used in conjunction with the Health and Safety at Work, etc Act 1974 to determine compliance with the law. From 1.10.89 these, in turn, will be replaced by Maximum Exposure Limits (MELs) or Occupational Exposure Standards (OESs) which are an integral part of the statutory control framework for hazardous substances written into COSHH.

Introduction

The use of the law as a means of controlling behaviour is some-thing with which we are all familiar. The speed at which we travel on the roads and the age at which we can legally con-sume intoxicating drinks on licensed premises are good everyday examples of where the law has drawn the line. Wher-ever you have lines separating the law-abiding from the wrongdoers you have difficult questions to deal with when, tak-ing the above examples, the speed is only just over the prescribed limit, or the under-age drinker is only a few days short of the legal age. It is the function of the courts to dispense justice in every case, including the borderline ones, and take into account all mitigating circumstances before deciding what action to take. What are the difficulties that confront the law-makers when they seek to draw lines to determine how much contamination can be allowed in the workplace?

Individual susceptibilities to atmospheric contaminants differ enormously. What has severe consequences for one worker may scarcely affect another. Whose reaction should be chosen as a reference point for drawing safe or dangerous limits? It could be said that choosing an average position is still unfair to the highly susceptible worker and gives the least susceptible worker a degree of protection he or she apparently does not need, almost certainly at considerable financial cost to the em-ployer.

Consider synergism — roughly speaking this is the effect of one harmful agent being added to the effect of a second harm-ful agent with the result that their combined effect is greater than the sum of their individual effects. The classic example of synergism in the field of occupational health is the habit of cigarette smoking and the exposure to asbestos dust. An asbes-tos worker who is a medium/heavy smoker is far more likely to contract lung cancer than an asbestos worker who has never smoked. Such a worker is also more likely to contract lung cancer than an equivalent smoker who is not exposed to asbestos.

Add to these factors the considerable uncertainty that still exists about the short-, medium- and long-term toxicological effects of the exposure of workers to a wide range of substan-ces and it can be appreciated that knowing where to draw a precise line reflecting the boundary between what is dangerous and what is safe in the workplace in absolute terms is not difficult — it is impossible.

Nevertheless a line must be drawn if the legislators are going to provide the precision which every law must have. If the law is not precise it is not only bad, because of its vagueness, but also unenforceable.

The past

In comprehending future methods of statutory control, it is helpful to have a general grasp of how things have been dealt with in the past.

Take, for example, the regulations enacted in 1911 to control the hazards from lead in the lead smelting industry. Readers of the short, nineteen clause regulations (now revoked) would have sought in vain for any numerical indication of what would have been accepted as compliance. There were the usual requirements for protective clothing, respirators, suitable mealrooms and washing facilities, but no level of contamination capable of scientific measurement is cited. Everything turned on the effectiveness of the ventilation system made obligatory for all the fume-producing processes. These, said the law, had to be undertaken with "efficient exhaust draught". The criterion of efficiency was crude and empirical "no draught shall be deemed efficient which fails to remove smoke generated at the point where such gas, vapour, fumes or dust originate". The more reliable indicators of success or failure in lead control were the results of the monthly medical examinations of the exposed lead workers. This was backed up by the doctor's power to suspend those who, in his or her opinion, would be involved in "special danger" to their health if they continued working with lead.

Not all lead workers were within the scope of the industry and process-based regulations. Those who were not covered by them had only the protection of the general duty in s.63 of the Factories Act 1961 (and its similarly worded predecessors). This said that if dust or fumes or other impurities were given off in any process and they were likely to be injurious or offensive, all practicable measures had to be taken to protect workers against inhaling the toxic material. Again, there was no reference to what was regarded as toxic, or at what point the concentration of toxic contaminant overstepped the mark between legality and illegality.

Threshold Limits

In the 1970s the British authorities chose to use the figures compiled by the American Conference of Governmental Industrial Hygienists (ACGIH). These figures were called Threshold Limit Values (TLVs) and the definition given for them was as follows:

> Threshold limit values refer to airborne concentrations of substances and represent conditions under which it is believed that nearly all workers may be repeatedly exposed day after day without adverse affect.

The definition goes on to repeat what has been written earlier, namely that individuals vary in their susceptibility to toxicants and some may have pre-existing physical conditions which make them vulnerable at contamination levels below the given TLV. In some cases the hypersensitive may be identified by the use of suitable tests. They may be guided into non-hazardous environments. Where an employer knows of a condition in an employee which makes him or her more susceptible to injury, or makes the consequences of injury more severe than usual, the employer must take extra precautions. This was established in the case of *Paris v Stepney Borough Council* [1951] 1 All ER 42, HL [1951] AC 36.

Mr Paris was a man who had already been blinded in one eye during the war. His accident, whilst using a hammer to loosen a U-bolt under a truck, happened when a piece of metal flew off and blinded his good eye. In the judgement, Lord Moreton of Henryton said "The duty to take reasonable precautions against injury is one which is owed by the employer to every individual workman".

Caveats to the use of Occupational Exposure Limits

As soon as a legal enforcement regime is linked to a set of

figures, however tenuously, a number of caveats are usually presented. The first is that the exposure limit, a figure given either in parts per million (ppm) of the contaminant in air, or in mg/m3, is not a sharp dividing line between dangerous and safe. Normally exposure limits are time-weighted averages spread over an 8 hour day or 40 hour week, so excursions above the specified limit are in fact contemplated. TLV-TWA was the abbreviation for Threshold Limit Value-Time Weighted Average. Some fast-acting substances, however, used to be given what were termed ceiling limits (TLV-C). These were limits which were never to be exceeded.

Between the TLV-TWA and TLV-C was a middle category, the TLV Short Term Exposure Limit (TLV-STEL). This gave a concentration to which workers could have been exposed for up to 15 minutes. It is set below the level which produces intolerable irritation; chronic or irreversible tissue change; or, narcosis likely to induce accidents; impair self-rescue; or reduce work efficiency. Such exposures were limited to four in any day with at least an hour between them. The TWA-STEL limits were also operated within the constraints of the daily TLV-TWA figures for the substance concerned.

In the USA, where the TLV Figures of the ACGIH are published annually, they still serve as guidelines to good practice. Where they are also used in Federal and State statutes and registers they assume the force of law.

Before moving to the future, a number of further observations are necessary and these have always assumed a place of prominence in the published literature on both sides of the Atlantic. The first and a vitally important one, is that which states very clearly that because the name of a substance is not to be found in the list it must not be assumed that exposure to that substance is safe. To give some perspective to the matter, some figures which emerged in May 1983 at the 10th World Congress on the Prevention of Occupational Accidents and Diseases in Ottawa, are relevant. There are approximately 600,000 chemical substances used in the world today. In only about 1200 instances do international standards exist giving control levels of workplace exposure. The ACGIH list includes just over half this number.

As a result of continuing epidemiological and animal experiment work, the list changes from time to time and the TLVs are revised. More often that not the concentration limits are reduced as research reveals more evidence of adverse effects. The reverse, where research reveals less reason for concern about ill-effects, is very infrequent.

The final point about the use of figures, which has to be stressed, concerns their interpretation. Any assessment of contaminants and the extent, location and type of the escape should be undertaken by a competent professional occupational hygienist.

He or she will not only be able to advise on the occupational health aspects of any identification and measurement work (dealt with more fully in later chapters), but will also be able to suggest conservation and waste reduction measures that will be worthwhile financially. This positive aspect of the work of an occupational hygienist is seldom put on the credit side of the balance sheet. It should be.

TLVs were used as guides in Great Britain from the mid-1970s. As time went along, a number of differences and alternative standards appeared on this side of the Atlantic so the necessity for provisos and explanations prior to the use of the ACGIH tables of figures increased. The American figures were published annually by the Health and Safety Executive in one of its Environmental Health Guidance Notes. The last annual revision of the Guidance Note in its old form appeared with the 1980 American figures, which were published in 1981.

Occupational Exposure Limits

The position from 1984 was that Great Britain had, for the first time, its own Occupational Exposure Limits (OELs). These were divided into two groups. The first group, with only a handful of figures, consisted of Control Limits; the second, much larger, group consisted of Recommended Limits.

Before commenting on the then new concept it is necessary to describe how TLVs were used in relation to the legal requirements which changed so fundamentally with the coming into force of the Health and Safety at Work, etc Act 1974 (HSWA) on 1.4.75.

What did the Act require in relation to workplace contamination by airborne toxicants? The key requirement was in s.2 of the Act. Every employer had to ensure the health of his or her employees "so far as is reasonably practicable". Ss.3 and 4 of the Act extended the same duty to cover the protection of everyone else who might be affected (eg: visitors, neighbours and members of the public). The way that an employer fulfilled the duty was largely left to him or her to determine. Even if Approved Codes of Practice (ACOPs) ie: codes of practice formally approved by the Health and Safety Commission, specified a particular route of control or regime of precautions, it was always open to an employer to choose a different route or regime. The only drawback, which some might have found if they chose the route not specified in the Approved Code, was that the burden of proving that their chosen method was as good as, or better than, the one officially blessed, fell upon them.

This left the qualifying phrase "so far as is reasonably practicable" to be examined. What did it mean? The Court of Appeal had given its judgement on the matter. *Edwards v National Coal Board* [1949] IKB 704, [1949] 1 All ER 743, 65 TLR 430, CA. If you had to do something "so far as is reasonably practicable" you had first to weigh up and analyse the hazard concerned. Its seriousness and its probability both needed to be looked at. You then weighed up all the factors involved with getting rid of the hazard or controlling it effectively. The greater the hazard and risk (ie: the probability or chance of it becoming manifest), the greater the burden before the duty of doing all that was reasonably practicable was discharged.

It was firmly believed that if airborne contaminants were the issue, then the establishment, as a matter of evidence, that the environmental contamination was within the published limits went a long way towards satisfying a court that all that was reasonably practicable was being done. If this were not the case it is considered that published figures would have been seriously flawed and their credibility dangerously undermined.

Consultations on proposals for new regulations

In 1984 the Health and Safety Commission (HSC) published a

consultative document called "Control of Substances Hazardous to Health". In it, the HSC declared that it believed earlier legislative controls in relation to occupational health had been limited in scope, both as to where they applied and also to the processes to which they applied. Furthermore, the requirements of the Health and Safety at Work, etc Act 1974, and in particular s.2, were such general requirements that obligations put upon employers and employees were not always clearly understood.

In addition, HSC stated that the law which existed was unnecessarily complex; inhibited the introduction of new technology to control health risks; was inadequate to allow ratification by the United Kingdom of the ILO Convention on Carcinogenic Substances and Agents; did not provide a suitable infra-structure to implement EC directives as and when they were adopted and had to be implemented by Member States.

On the matter of the size of the country's occupational health problem, the HSC cited some figures from the Department of Health and Social Security (as it then was). In 1979-1980 DHSS had awarded over 5700 new injury benefits for short spells of incapacity, 850 new longer-term disablement benefits and 710 death benefits. In terms of working days lost, by the absences attributable to the figures given above, the total amount, in round figures, was 187,000 working days. Chronic bronchitis, asthma and emphysema (a condition in which the air sacs of the lungs are grossly enlarged causing breathlessness and wheezing) may or may not be occupationally linked. In 1980, however, from these three causes there were 20,000 deaths and over 30 million lost working days. Some of the cases must have originated in the workplace. Other cases caused elsewhere may have been exacerbated by hostile conditions in the workplace. Yet other cases, of course, were conditions contracted independently of the workplace and having no connection with work activities whatsoever. No one knows where the dividing line lies.

Except for mesothelioma and bladder cancer, DHSS statistics do not cover cancer which *may* be occupationally linked. A review in the USA in the 1970s estimated occupationally related cancers amounted to up to 30% of all cancer deaths. A recent United Kingdom study put the figure at 2 - 8% of cancers having occupational links.

In 1980 there were 130,000 cancer deaths, so even if the

truth lies closer to the lower than to the higher figure we may be looking at between 10,000 - 15,000 occupationally linked cancer deaths per year.

All these figures indicate a problem of considerable dimensions, so the COSHH proposals were timely. In essence, the aim with COSHH was to produce one set of regulations stating broad principles to be followed. They had to be flexible enough to accommodate changes made necessary by hazards newly discovered, by advances in control technology and by new EC directives and ILO conventions. Furthermore, the new regulations were to simplify existing law and enable obsolete law to be repealed or revoked.

What was absolutely certain was that a crucial part of the adequacy of every control regime would be the part played by Occupational Exposure Limits, a subject developed more fully in the next chapter.

Chapter 3

Exposure limits

Officially published lists of exposure limits do not cover all substances, but those which are published each year reflect current medical and scientific knowledge concerning several hundred of those in more common use. Users are required to know the potential for causing harm of all the materials they use. They can obtain indications of this from suppliers' data and labels. Users must also keep exposure to hazardous substances to the lowest level which is reasonably practicable. COSHH includes two classes of occupational exposure limits: Maximum Exposure Limits (MELs) and Occupational Exposure Standards (OESs), which each have a different legal status.

Background

The background to the use of numerical limits for indicating the boundary between what is safe to breathe at work and what is not, was touched on in the last chapter.

Here we examine developments more closely, stressing as we do that the caveats applicable to the old limits still apply to the new ones which have superseded them. The occupational exposure limit is *not* an absolute or clear-cut automatic dividing line between danger and safety, or legality and illegality. The list is still woefully incomplete when compared with the total number of potentially harmful airborne contaminants that could be encountered in the nation's workplaces. Hence the non-appearance of a substance on the list is not to be regarded as a go-ahead to neglect simple engineering control precautions and common sense care. It just means that, as yet, not enough is known about the substance to warrant its appearance in a list. Because this can be applied to so many substances which may contaminate workplace atmospheres, all dusts and fumes should be regarded as suspect and controlled as far as possible.

Nevertheless, despite its fully acknowledged shortcomings, a list of occupational exposure limits is a working document that only the imprudent or ignorant will ignore. It is used by the enforcing authorities and influences them in arriving at a decision on the appropriate course of action they take when reviewing the options open to them in obtaining improvements for the protection of exposed workers. It will also be used as part of the criteria by which enforcers will assess compliance with COSHH.

Knowledge and ignorance

An important point to appreciate here is the way the law may look at what it considers employers should know, as opposed to what they actually know. In an area where changes are not only possible but likely, it will not be a good enough defence to a charge brought before the courts for an employer to plead ignorance of, say, a halving of an occupational exposure limit applicable to any substance he or she is handling. Employers will be expected to take steps ·to keep themselves informed. The law takes what it expects the reasonable man to know as its yardstick both in deciding culpability and liability. The law expects the reasonable person to know about the processes he or she carries out at work and this includes knowing about any hazards that may be associated with those processes. Furthermore, if a reasonable person, for any reason, could not be expected to know, then he or she is expected to obtain and follow expert advice from others who specialise in the field and who have made it their business to know. In other words, employers handling, transporting, storing or involved in any way in using substances which may be harmful, must constantly take steps to keep themselves informed of the nature and extent of any hazard found to exist with them.

This picture is not as bleak, nor the task as demanding, as it may seem at first sight, because s.6 of the Health and Safety at Work, etc Act 1974, as amended by the Consumer Protection Act 1987, puts duties on manufacturers and suppliers of substances for use at work, to provide adequate information on hazards associated with the substances they supply and also keep that information up to date. In addition it further requires the same people to undertake research to reduce and, if possible, eliminate any hazards to which the substance may give rise. Clearly suppliers can not alter the inherent risks associated with any particular chemical they supply but they can and they should inform users about any conditions necessary to ensure safety and freedom from risks to health when the substance concerned is being properly used. It has been pointed out that the duty on suppliers was only to make available the information but increasingly they were actively disseminating their data to their customers because without it they (ie: the suppliers) may have been running some risk of not being able to take advantage of the "improper use" escape clause. This simply means that suppliers do not wait to be asked by a user for information. They supply it automatically thereby ensuring that the user knows what proper use of the particular substance is. Improper use is construed as use which is contrary to the supplier's reasonable instructions. Where improper use by a customer is established a supplier ceases to carry responsibility. This distinction no longer applies because of the changes to the wording of s.6 brought about by the Consumer Protection Act 1987, s.36 and schedule 3. Whereas before the changes the manufacturers or suppliers had the rather negative duty to make available adequate information to the users about the health and safety issues associated with the substances concerned, they now have a positive duty to provide the information.

Increasingly too, as commented on in Chapter 4, more existing substances are becoming subject to statutory labelling requirements which indicate the existence of hazards, their nature and severity. There is also the fairly recent regime dealing with new substances as they come onto the market. In Great Britain the Notification of New Substances Regulations 1982 came into force on 26.11.82. They implement EC directives dealing with dangerous substances. The purpose of the regulations is to ensure that the potential of a new chemical substance to cause harm to man and his environment is assessed *before* it is placed on the European Community market.

Reasonable practicability

Before looking at the limits themselves reference must again be made to the only qualification on the duty of an employer to ensure (ie: make certain of) the health of his or her employees and others — the qualification of reasonable practicability. It has already been said authoritatively by the Court of Appeal that the greater the degree of risk (ie: the lower the figures listed in the context of a book about exposure limits) the less weight will be given by the courts to the cost of measures needed to avoid or control the hazard. What is more, this issue of cost has nothing to do with the financial status of the employer. This is not a case of one law for the rich and another for the poor. The risk/cost equation is the same for rich and poor alike: it could not logically or legally be any other way. In the case of *Marshall v Gotham Co Ltd* [1954] AC 360, [1954] All ER 937, the House of Lords affirmed the decision of the Court of Appeal in the case of *Edwards v National Coal Board* (see page 29.) In the judgement Lord Reid said:

If a precaution is practicable it must be taken, unless in the whole circumstances that would be unreasonable. And, as men's lives may be at stake, it should not lightly be held that to take a practicable precaution is unreasonable...

Control limits and recommended limits

What then is a control limit and what is a recommended limit? How do they differ from previous figures and how are they integrated into workplace regimes and procedures? Despite the changes in description and status shortly to be made when COSHH takes effect, it is appropriate to have an understanding of what had gone on between 1984 and the present time.

Control Limits

Control Limits are those which the Health and Safety Commission has formally adopted. Readers will appreciate that the Health and Safety Commission is the body set up by the Health and Safety at Work, etc Act 1974 to advise Government on policy matters in the field of occupational health and safety and that the Health and Safety Executive is its enforcing arm sharing enforcement duties with local authorities under various pieces of legislation.

Prior to adopting any figure as a Control Limit (some of which may appear in an Approved Code of Practice, approved by the Health and Safety Commission with the consent of the Secretary of State and having special significance as evidence provided to support legal proceedings) the Health and Safety Commission will have satisfied itself, by reference to its specialist advisers, that the limits set represent a level of exposure "which it is reasonably practicable for all employers to achieve in all sectors of industry". The level of exposure set will also be that above which *the available medical evidence suggests there is a likely risk to health*.

Failure to keep atmospheric contamination below the published level will be regarded as prima facie evidence of the commission of a criminal offence. Those found guilty of such an offence are subject to a maximum fine not exceeding £2000 in the Magistrates Courts, or to an unlimited fine if the case is taken on indictment in the Crown Courts. Because of the history of relatively low levels of fines imposed in the lower courts there is a deliberate and increasingly common tendency for the authorities to take their cases on indictment where the higher penalties apply.

Recommended Limits

Recommended Limits are those exposure limits recommended by the Health and Safety Commission following the advice of ACTS (the Advisory Committee on Toxic Substances). They describe the exposure limits believed to represent good practice and to offer realistic criteria for the control of exposure in terms of engineering controls, supplemented where necessary by the appropriate personal protective clothing and respiratory protective equipment. Recommended Limits should be regarded much as Threshold Limits (TLVs) have been regarded in the past. Those who fail to establish and maintain control procedures and equipment which keep the atmospheric contamination to a level below that recommended, may also find themselves subject to some enforcement action.

A number of issues call for some clarification at this point. The first relates to the case where a Control Limit may legitimately be exceeded, despite what has been said earlier. An example occurs with lead in paragraph 2 of Appendix 1 of the Approved Code of Practice accompanying the Control of Lead at Work Regulations 1980. Here it states:

As the extent of lead absorption is related not only to the amount of lead present but also to factors such as composition, solubility, particle size and period of exposure, some departure from the lead-in-air standard may be allowed for the purposes of regulation 6 and 7 provided that (a) there is sufficient information available from biological test results to indicate that the degree of lead absorption is at an acceptable level; (b) 8 hour time-weighted average concentrations do not exceed 3 times the standard set out in paragraph 1 ie: lead (except for tetraethyl lead) (as Pb) 0.15mg/m3 of air.

The lead example shows as well as any that the use of figures is not quite as straightforward as we would like it to be.

After considering a permitted excursion over the control limit, it is thought pertinent to ask if, once levels have been reduced to a point below the published limit, anything else remains to be done. The answer is yes, there is.

A Control Limit is not a safe limit. It is an upper limit or permitted exposure and it is not holy writ. Usually it has no inherent separate legal status unless specifically written into statutory regulations. It should be understood that there still remains the statutory duty under s.2 of the Health and Safety at Work, etc Act 1974 to reduce exposure to the lowest reasonably practicable level *below the set upper limit*. Only when the cost of further reduction in exposure levels is disproportionate, is the criterion of reasonable practicability satisfied and the full legal obligation discharged. What may be considered to be disproportionate will always be a matter for debate and only capable of resolution in the last resort by the courts in the circumstances of the particular case. This reinforces the comments made earlier about the importance of the interpretation of figures being vested in professionally trained and experienced occupational hygiene practitioners. The above situation will change under COSHH as described later.

Another issue which needs to be explored is the relative toxicity of some of the substances appearing on the Control Limit list and others appearing on the list of Recommended Limits. It will appear paradoxical but it is nevertheless the case that there are substances on the Recommended Limit list which are in many ways nastier than some of those on the Control Limit list. The apparent lack of logic in this is explicable only when it is realised that the distinction between items appearing on the former list and items appearing on the latter is a pragmatic one, related to feasibility and practicability and not to toxicological factors.

Control Limits and Recommended Limits relate to airborne concentrations and, as has already been pointed out, breathing in a toxic substance, whilst the commonest route of entry, is not the only one. Other entry routes call for consideration and matters of protective clothing, prohibiting smoking and the partaking of food and drink, have to be thought about with the other precautions.

Safe levels

There are some substances for which there are significant reservations about any level being safe. This is particularly the case with substances suspected of being carcinogenic, teratogenic or mutagenic (ie: causing or predisposing to cancer, birth deformities, or genetic changes). No attempt has been made in this book to comment on the correctness of the levels set either as Control Limits or Recommended Limits. It is the case, however, that some people believe that in some instances the figures are set unnecessarily low and that those who abide by them suffer an unnecessary and unjustifiable cost penalty which may affect their competitiveness. Equally, other figures are believed to be set at too high a level. These issues, whilst important politically, are not within the scope of this guide.

An interesting development relevant to the setting of an Occupational Exposure Limit was that involving asbestos and the points made in what has become known as the Grant Report. Grant was one of the HSE's Area Directors who chaired a working group given the job of identifying and recommending any further measures for asbestos dust control not considered practicable when the Advisory Committee on Asbestos produced its final report in 1979. Grant reported to HSC in mid-1983 and some of his group's comments are most relevant to the appreciation of the difficulties which can be encountered in the process of setting exposure levels, more especially where there is no recognised safe level. Asbestos dust, by statutory definition, said Grant, is "dust consisting of or containing asbestos to such an extent as is liable to cause danger to the health of employed persons". Because current medical evidence has indicated there is no threshold below which exposure to asbestos is safe, those who had to comply with the Asbestos Regulations 1969 had a straightforward choice. They either had to exclude totally all asbestos dust from their workplaces, which is a practical impossibility, or they had to equip all workers exposed to asbestos with approved respiratory protective equipment and protective clothing and ensure it was used.

Now, said Grant, there may be a risk of injury below "the lowest quantifiable level". Therefore dust liable to cause danger to health would be less than that which HSE guidance describes as an upper limit of permitted exposure. This, complained Grant's group, put forward a Control Limit which was not "safe" but was nevertheless "permitted" — a state of affairs outside both the spirit and the letter of the law. Grant's group advanced the concept of an action level to overcome the difficulty. An action level would set a point at which the Asbestos Regulations 1969 would be deemed to take effect. It would not be a ceiling limit because it conceded there would be places where the action level could not be achieved. Bringing an action level "into line with the legal definition of dust in the

Asbestos Regulations 1969 would be the most effective single measure which could now be taken to control inhalation of asbestos dust". It is a "single, logical, legal and defensible regime of control" which is wanted, said the Grant report. Making so much fuss of a Control Limit, intimates Grant, encourages people to cease their efforts once the workplace concentration has been brought below the stipulated exposure limit. The group contended that a stage had been reached where the "teeth of the Asbestos Regulations have been effectively extracted by well intentioned guidance".

The HSC gave careful consideration to what the Grant Report recommended ie: that there should be an action level below which the Asbestos Regulations should not apply. They announced in November 1983, however, that they had chosen to follow the ACTS approach, adopted by the European Community Asbestos (Worker Protection) Directive, and not to accede to Grant's proposals. This, they said, will ensure that there is a continuing and overriding requirement to reduce exposure to a level as low as reasonably practicable.

Enforcement policy

EH40 "Occupational Exposure Limits", HSE's Guidance Note on its new policy, stated clearly, after the customary reservation mentioned earlier, that only the courts can give binding decisions on interpretation in particular cases, that it will work on the basis that exposure limits, which may be embodied in regulations; Approved Codes of Practice; EC directives; or, simply adopted by the Health and Safety Commission and only to be found published in EH40, *should not normally be exceeded.* Failure to comply with limits or to reduce exposure further within the bounds of reasonable practicability, will predispose them towards enforcement action either through the serving of improvement or prohibition notices, or prosecution or both.

Further, the HSE does not distinguish between long and short term exposure limits (described later) for enforcement purposes. In other words it is no more excusable to allow a short term limit to be exceeded than a long term limit, because such a limit is based on physiological and toxicological issues and not on whether a lapse of control measures is momentary or chronic. Rigid interpretation of figures will never be implicit in the role of enforcement in the future, but it must be understood that the burden of establishing reasonable practicability will fall entirely on the shoulders of those having to control airborne contamination. Flexibility is different from leniency in enforcement; it is important to realise this and not to muddle the two.

In this connection however one thing is fairly certain, the newly presented occupational exposure limits will feature as a very important factor. Take, for example, the prohibition notice. This may only be served where the inspector concerned is of the opinion that an activity or process "will involve a risk of serious personal injury" (a defined term in s.53 to mean "any disease and any impairment of a person's physical or mental condition"). Where will inspectors turn to satisfy, themselves in the first instance and a court or tribunal later on, that their opinions are soundly based? The answer is EH40 and the published limit for the substance concerned.

Recommended limits will be used as yardsticks in plant design, including the design of such control devices as filters and local exhaust ventilation equipment. The limit reflects good practice. If higher standards of control are achieved then this will reflect a commensurate degree of excellence. If lower standards are found then remonstrance and recrimination may follow both from the customer buying the plant and/or from the enforcing inspector. Until now however, HSE has not adopted an overtly very aggressive enforcement policy on new plant and equipment design under s.6 of the Health and Safety at Work, etc Act 1974. Despite much behind-the-scenes discussions and consultation on design improvements in plant, many believe a much tougher enforcement line should have been taken.

Occupational Exposure Limits

The tables printed in EH40/89 show the long-term exposure limit (an eight hour time-weighted figure) and a short-term exposure limit (a ten minute time-weighted figure, considered to be the shortest feasible sampling period).

In each case there is usually an entry showing the limit in parts per million (ppm). This is a measure of concentration by volume. There is also usually an entry showing milligrams per cubic metre of air (mg m^3). Non-particulate gases and vapours normally have their limits expressed in ppm and particulate contaminants in the measure of concentration by mass (ie: mg m^3). Asbestos fibres are an exception, their limits are expressed as fibres per millilitre of air (fibres ml^1).

Although the Guidance Note concerns itself almost exclusively with airborne contaminants, other factors enter the arena when monitoring workers' exposure. As indicated already with the example about lead, biological monitoring is part of what employers are called upon to do to show they are in compliance.

Why both long-term and short-term figures? The reason as indicated, is related to the range of toxicological responses described in Chapter 1. Some substances produce almost immediate symptoms of damage and distress. For the type of substance producing such acute effects the short-term exposure limit (STEL) is highly relevant. Other substances accumulate during the long latent period between the beginning of exposure and the onset of symptoms. For this type of substance the long-term limit is appropriate because it concerns total intake over an extended period.

The STEL is based on the ten minute period, thought to be the shortest time for which sampling is realistic. Anything shorter than ten minutes would probably not register peaks as a general rule. It has been this practical problem which has prompted the abandonment of the use of ceiling limits (designated by the capital letter C) which the American ACGIH still uses in its TLV list. Whilst it is recognised that there are certain short-term exposure concentrations, or ceiling limits, which ought not to be exceeded at all at any time, there is little point in maintaining the idea, if a ten minute period is the shortest feasible period for which an acceptable and reliable measurement can be taken. Where existing technology does enable shorter sampling times to be used the HSE guidance will indicate accordingly.

Now that the concept of the exposure limit has been explored and the way that it has been used in enforcement has been described it is almost time to turn to practical matters of identification, measurement procedures and management. It is to these subjects that the remainder of the book is devoted.

Before doing so, a note on the transitional period between

the present day and the date when COSHH takes effect is appropriate.

When COSHH comes into operation on 1.10.89 the terms Control Limit and Recommended Limit will disappear. They will, however, remain as terms of significance up until 30.9.89 and also in any legal proceedings or litigation commenced before 1 October and continuing after that date. Only when all such matters have been disposed of will the terms Control Limit and Recommended Limit finally cease to be relevant.

The role of Occupational Exposure Limits in COSHH

Before dwelling on the specific role and status of Occupational Exposure Limits in the Control of Substances Hazardous to Health Regulations 1988 it is essential to understand the philosophy and principles which lie behind the regulations themselves.

Throughout the remainder of the chapter, where the text is covered by a relevant requirement in COSHH or where the Approved Code of Practice explains it or expands upon it, a reference is given.

The regulations, which will govern the statutory control of occupational health for many years to come, are based primarily on a conditional prohibition. This will operate from 1.10.89 in the following way.

No employer will be able, after that date, to employ anyone on work which is liable to expose them to any substances hazardous to their health (regulation 2 and 6(1)), *unless* he or she has made a suitable and sufficient assessment of the risks created by such exposure *and* of the steps needed to be taken to comply with the requirements of the regulations.

Assessments

In most instances the initial assessment, which except in the very simplest of cases has to be recorded (ACOP paragraph 20), must also be reviewed if its validity is ever suspect or if a significant change is made in the nature of the work (ACOP paragraph 22).

An assessment's validity could be called into question if the results of the required tests of engineering controls (regulation 9) proved to be unsatisfactory at any time, or if workplace exposure monitoring indicated inadequacies in the control measures, eg: fans inadequate or dust captor-hoods wrongly placed, broken, or of poor design.

Similarly, if health surveillance procedures (regulation 11), including those involving biological monitoring undertaken by a medical practitioner, confirmed a case of occupationally induced disease (eg: mercury absorption established by the testing of a urine sample), or if new information appeared about the nature of a relevant health risk (ACOP paragraph 23) a reassessment would be legally required.

Whatever the assessment shows to be necessary to prevent or adequately control the exposure of employees to hazardous substances will have to be done to comply with the law. COSHH calls for whatever is necessary to protect employee's health from the hazardous substances to which they are liable to be exposed at work.

Following the assessment there is a series of mandatory steps to be taken by the employer (regulation 7):

(a) Exposure to hazardous substances should be *prevented*.

(b) Where prevention is not reasonably practicable, it is permissible if *adequate control* is exercised.

(c) *Measures other than personal protective equipment* must be used to achieve prevention or adequate control.

(d) Where (a) and (b) are insufficient by themselves to achieve control, the employer must provide *suitable personal protective equipment* to achieve it.

Occupational Exposure Limits

So what, might one ask, is adequate control achieved by whatever combination of the above?

The answer lies with the newly named Maximum Exposure Limits and Occupational Exposure Standards. Both terms, shortened to MEL and OES, are defined in COSHH (regulation 2).

A Maximum Exposure Limit relates presently to only those 29 substances listed in schedule 1 of COSHH. However, since the statutory instrument was made in September 1988 a further substance has been added to the list (acrylamide — with effect from 1.7.89), and another substance has had its MEL halved (arsenic — with effect from 1.1.89). In the future it is expected that there will be a steady trickle of additions and changes.

Maximum Exposure Limits (MELs)

Where a substance with an MEL can be inhaled, control will only be treated as being adequate if the level of exposure is reduced "so far as is reasonably practicable and in any case *below the maximum exposure limit*". Why, having achieved the MEL, must an employer do more? The answer is simple and straightforward. The MEL is *not* a safe limit. It is a limit set by the Health and Safety Commission, on the advice of its Advisory Committee on Toxic Substances (ACTS), at a level which has been judged to be reasonably practicable for the whole spectrum of work activities in Great Britain.

Occupational Exposure Standards (OESs)

Where there is exposure to a substance with an OES, the control will be treated as adequate, as far as inhalation is concerned, if the OES is not exceeded. Alternatively, where it is exceeded but the employer knows why and is taking action "as soon as reasonably practicable" this will also be treated as adequate control.

As a result of the "reasonably practicable" qualification it is employers who bear the burden of proof "on the balance of probabilities" where they contend that their remedies meet the needs of the particular case.

Where respiratory protective equipment is covered and the option of using it is allowable (ie: the employer can show that neither prevention nor adequate control by means other than personal protective equipment is reasonably practicable) the adequacy is related to suitability for purpose and approved by the Health and Safety Executive.

Chapter 4

Identifying the contaminants

Written information, observations, and worker symptoms may all indicate potential hazards. All should be noted, as should official and other standard reference works and available computerised data on the toxicity of materials. Medical surveillance may be advisable as a routine added check on worker health but direct workplace evidence of contamination should always be sought. Sources of visible dust should be tracked down and the sense of smell utilised, notwithstanding its drawbacks. All the above matters are relevant to the making of the statutory assessment required by COSHH.

Dilemma

In preparing a monitoring programme for chemical contaminants, there appears to be a dilemma. If harmful levels of chemicals are present they must be measured but how are they known to be harmful until they are measured? This chapter is about indications that atmospheric contamination may require further attention, without actually undertaking the complex measurements which are dealt with more fully in the next chapter.

Broadly speaking, a detailed study of chemical contamination is likely to be prompted by one of three possible observations. Firstly, written information may indicate that the substances in use could be hazardous. Under s.6 of the Health and Safety at Work, etc Act 1974 and the Classification, Packaging and Labelling of Dangerous Substances Regulations 1984 (usually referred to simply as the CPL Regulations), there are statutory duties relating to the display and provision of such information. These are described further below. Secondly, employees in the workplace may be enquiring, complaining, or even experiencing symptoms which might have an occupational cause. Thirdly, observations of occurrences which are not in themselves hazardous, could nevertheless indicate possible contamination of the environment. Examples of phenomena in this third category are smells, corrosion or staining of plant, equipment or the structure or the building, and visible dust.

Written information

In theory at any rate, written information is available about the hazards of all substances supplied for use at work. The duty to provide such information is imposed upon those who manufacture or supply substances, by s.6 (4) of the Health and Safety at Work, etc Act 1974. The requirements are:

(a) to ensure, so far as is reasonably practicable, that the substance is safe and without risks to health when properly used;

(b) to carry out or arrange for the carrying out of such testing and examination as may be necessary for the performance of the duty imposed by the preceding paragraph;

(c) to take such steps as are necessary to secure that there will be available, in connection with the use of the substance at work, adequate information about the results of any relevant tests which have been carried out on, or in connection with the substance, and about any conditions necessary to ensure that it will be safe and without risks to health when properly used.

The duty was made more stringent by the amendments to s.6 effected by s.36 and schedule 3 of the Consumer Protection Act 1987, which came into effect on 1.3.88. The Act replaced the requirement for the making available of information with a more positive requirement to secure that persons supplied with articles or substances *are provided with* adequate information about them. Furthermore, revisions of the information must also be provided if it becomes known that anything gives rise to a serious risk to health or safety.

In addition, s.6 (5) of the Health and Safety at Work, etc Act 1974 requires the manufacturers of substances for use at work to carry out, or arrange for the carrying out, of any necessary research with a view to the discovery and, so far as is reasonably practicable, the elimination or minimisation of any risks to health and safety to which the substance may give rise.

These requirements, as noted earlier, were further reinforced by the Notification of New Substances Regulations 1982. This implements an EC directive to ensure that specific hazard data on new substances on the EC market in quantities greater than one tonne per year is submitted for inclusion in an inventory (EINECS) compiled by the European Commission.

Thus, much the most straightforward way to obtain information about the hazards of substances in the workplace is to obtain information required by law. If the manufacturer of the substance is based in the United Kingdom, he or she is probably the best source of information. However, if the manufacturer is overseas and not bound by the Health and Safety at Work, etc Act 1974, the information must be made available by the supplier or the importer.

The provision of information can give rise to problems. The most likely problem is that the information provided is found to be unsatisfactory for some reason. The information may be too complex to understand readily or, on the other hand, it may be too general or simple to be useful, with phrases like "avoid inhaling the fumes" or "use in a ventilated area". The user may also be concerned that the manufacturer is unlikely to be sufficiently objective to highlight the hazards of the product. A study undertaken by Social Audit, based on research carried out in 1978 and 1979, concluded that, although there were many exceptions, suppliers' data sheets could not be regarded as a consistently reliable or accurate source of information.

This problem cannot necessarily be solved completely but it can be minimised by specifying to the manufacturer exactly what information is wanted. A number of organisations, notably trade unions, have prepared lists of information to request from manufacturers. Some of these would be daunting to even the most conscientious supplier, but clearly the user is entitled to quite specific answers to the following questions:

    (a)   What level, if any, of the substance in the atmosphere is hazardous?

    (b)   What are the harmful effects of the substance?

    (c)   Are there any known long term (chronic) effects of exposure?

    (d)   How should atmospheric levels be measured?

    (e)   What is the first aid procedure following accidental exposure?

    (f)   What is the procedure for dealing with spillages?

    (g)   How should waste containing the substance be treated?

    (h)   What are the correct storage conditions?

    (i)   What protective clothing, or other measures, are required when handling the substance?

It should be noted that the above questions are those relevant to toxic hazard but the user may also wish to raise points concerning hazards such as fire and explosion, which are outside the scope of this book. It might also be appropriate to request information, if available, directly relevant to the intended conditions of use. This could include possible reactions with other substances and behaviour under particular conditions of temperature and pressure.

A further problem with hazard data provided by manufacturers, etc is that, even if adequate and accurate, the layout and terminology of the information is not standardised. It may therefore take some study before it is clearly understood and it is likely that any omissions will not be immediately obvious. There are pressing reasons for requiring that all information is provided in the same format, not least that the information may be required in an emergency when a familiar layout will assist speedy consultation. However, unless this becomes a legal requirement, users must represent the information themselves. The compilation of a loose-leaf manual of hazard data sheets in which the essential information is summarised on a single page is recommended. Such an inventory will form an ideal basis for the "sufficient and suitable" assessment required to be undertaken as part of COSHH.

Appropriate headings are:

Toxic hazard high/medium/low MEL...ppm mg m^{-3}
OES... ppm mg m^{-3}
Fire hazard high/medium/low Flash point...°C
Storage conditions
Protective clothing requirements
First aid procedure
Spillage procedure
Waste disposal procedure
Fire fighting procedure

MEL = Maximum Exposure Limit (COSHH regulation 2 and schedule 1)
OES = Occupational Exposure Standard (COSHH regulation 2 and EH40/89)

The emphasis in devising such data sheets should be to omit information of little relevance on a day to day basis (such as the LD50, the dose of the substance which kills 50% of a group of test animals) and to ensure that information which the user might actually need is provided. Completion of data sheets will rapidly demonstrate if important information is missing and will produce a document which can be quickly consulted by a wide range of personnel.

Labelling

The information discussed so far is that to which the user is legally entitled on request. However, it will not always be presented in the best form and it may well be necessary to look also to other sources of information, One of these is the warning label on the product.

At one time, such labels were a very uncertain guide to product hazards. They came in all shapes and sizes, or were non-existent and the wording followed no standard pattern. However, the Packaging and Labelling of Dangerous Substances Regulations 1978 require that approximately 800 listed substances were labelled with easily understood symbols. The symbols indicated graphically whether the substance was toxic, harmful or irritant, corrosive, explosive, highly flammable or oxidising. The limitation of the regulations was that a substance may have had dangerous properties which did not appear on the prescribed list.

In September 1984 the 1978 labelling regulations were replaced by the CPL Regulations which gave effect to a number of EC directives on the subject. The CPL Regulations make provision for the classification, packaging and labelling of dangerous substances both for supply and for conveyance by road. The supply provisions are designed specifically to offer protection to those who handle or use the dangerous substances, either at work or in the home. Whilst some substances are made specifically for use at work and others for use in the home, in very many instances they are used equally in both.

This is achieved by labels which warn users of the immediate and the longer-term potential hazards in what are called *risk phrases*. There are 48 of them and they are to be found in Part IV of the document referred to as the Approved List. The full title of the document, the second edition of which appeared in February 1988, is "Authorised and approved list — Information approved for the classification, packaging and labelling of dangerous substances for supply and conveyance by road".

A few of the risk phrases used relevant to COSHH are: "harmful by inhalation", "harmful in contact with skin", "very toxic if swallowed", "irritating to eyes", "may cause sensitisation by inhalation", "possible risk of irreversible effects", "may cause cancer", "may cause birth defects".

There are also 19 further categories of phrase where there are a combination of risks: "very toxic by inhalation, in contact with skin and if swallowed". There is no room for doubt with a substance labelled in this fashion that it needs to be handled with very great care.

Another important role of the Approved List is that where listed substances indicate the nature of the risk as "very toxic", toxic, harmful, corrosive or irritant" then those substances are, by definition, classed as "substances hazardous to health" within the meaning given to the phrase by COSHH (regulation 2).

Whilst Part IV can assist greatly in assessment (regulation 6), Part V containing 53 safety phrases can assist greatly in planning the strategy of prevention and adequate control (regulation 7). Examples of safety phrases pertinent to risks to health are: "when using do not smoke", "do not breathe dust", "wear suitable gloves", "if you feel unwell, seek medical advice (show the label where possible)", etc.

Other sources of information

The information considered so far is that provided by the manufacturer, importer, or supplier of the substance in question. In addition, there are many other sources of valuable information. The extent to which these are consulted will depend upon the degree of concern about possible hazards and the scale of use of the substance in question. However, in all cases it will be appropriate to consult the Health and Safety Executive's Occupational Exposure Limits.

These limits, described elsewhere, are contained in the Health and Safety Executive's Guidance Note EH40, published annually. The EH designation stands for Environmental Hygiene, which is one of the five categories of Guidance Note available to assist employers in complying with their statutory duties. Guidance Notes have no special status in themselves, as a rule, but they give an indication of what the prudent employer ought to know. Following a certain time after their appearance they become part of the fund of knowledge which an employer is deemed to know in the safe conduct of affairs at the workplace.

The 1989 edition has appeared earlier in the year than has hitherto been the case, so that those preparing for the advent of the Control of Substances Hazardous to Health Regulations 1988 have good time to conform with the new law when it takes effect on 1.10.89.

For the first time, despite what was stated above about Guidance Notes having no special status in themselves, EH40 is somewhat different because it repeats, as Table 1, the Maximum Exposure Limits taken from the COSHH Statutory

Instrument. Both Maximum Exposure Limits (MELs) and Occupational Exposure Standards (OESs) are an integral part of establishing the adequacy of control which Regulation 7 of COSHH calls for, where it has not proved reasonably practicable to prevent exposure of employees to substances hazardous to their health.

The introductory parts of EH40 are devoted to putting Occupational Exposure Limits into the context of COSHH. Then each of the four tables comprising the main part of EH40 are described.

Table 1 lists the Maximum Exposure Limits and is a reflection of schedule 1 of COSHH where 20 substances are named together with their long-term Maximum Exposure Limits (eight hour time weighted average reference period) and/or their short term Maximum Exposure Limits (ten minute reference period). The limits are given in parts per million (ppm), or milligrams per cubic metre (mg m^{-3}).

The significance of the two limits is that they tackle not only the long-term total intake of the body of the hazardous substances over long periods (long-term exposure limits) but also the avoidance of acute effects likely to appear after just brief exposures (short-term exposure limits). Unlike schedule 1 of COSHH, Table 1 of EH40 gives Skin Notations, represented by the letters SK for 12 out of the 29 listed substances to indicate that inhalation is not the only route into the body but that the toxic effects can also come about following absorption through the unbroken skin.

The other significant point to make about Table 1 is that because the substances there are accorded their legal status by their appearance in the Statutory Instrument itself, to make any changes involves changing the law.

This will entail a consultative document put out by the Health and Safety Commission: the appraisal of responses to the document by the HSC/HSE and a formal submission of proposed changes for the approval of the Secretary of State for the Department of Employment. This will be an annual event to accord MEL status to whatever substances are involved. At the time of writing HSC has already indicated changes for acrylamide and arsenic which will involve the new procedure.

Table 2 lists Occupational Exposure Standards. Table 3 put forward proposed changes to the Occupational Exposure Standard list and Table 4 lists those substances to be reviewed by the Health and Safety Commission's Advisory Committee on Toxic Substances (ACTS) and WATCH (Working group on the Assessment of Toxic Chemicals).

EH40 also covers special points relating to pesticides, dusts, fumes, allergenic sensitisers, percutaneous (skin) absorption and unlisted substances. The absence of a substance from the lists of MELs and OESs does not indicate it is safe. It merely indicates that not enough is known about it to warrant its inclusion. The Approved Code of Practice accompanying COSHH indicates the manner in which such substances should be dealt with by employers.

On the question of monitoring for the purposes of comparing actual exposure with limits set out in EH40, the Guidance Note advises the close study of its sister GN, EH42 "Monitoring Strategies for Toxic Substances".

For more detailed information, there are a number of standard textbooks which are very informative. For example, "Dangerous Properties of Industrial Materials" by N Irving Sax lists the main physical and toxicity data of more than 20,000 materials, together with a rating for known hazards in various categories such as toxic hazard and fire hazard. Further information on this and other useful references is given on pages 89–92.

Detailed information is available from the Health and Safety Executive in their Environmental Hygiene series of Guidance Notes and a list of the relevant ones in the series up to the time of publication is given in pages 87–88.

In addition, the Executive issue Toxicity Reviews from time to time which present an in-depth review of the literature and medical and scientific evidence concerning particular substances. Toxicity Reviews to date cover 19 substances which are listed on page 86.

For thorough searches of published information, it is worth considering the use of a computerised data base. The Health and Safety Executive have their own system HSELINE which searches references on a wide range of safety topics and is now available from Pergamon Infoline. The British Telecom system PRESTEL also contains a health and safety section. More specific chemical hazard data is available on American data bases such as TOXLINE and RTECS. Information on such systems can be obtained from BLAISE, the British Library Automated Information Service, 2 Sheraton Street, London W1V 4BH.

Since the first edition was published there has been what has been described as an "explosion of scientific information". Not only is the volume of such information very great and hence the cost of reviewing it efficiently very high, but its effective analysis to obtain what is needed calls for a wide range of different scientific disciplines which very few companies can draw upon from their own resources.

A further important source of chemical information is the appropriate trade or research association. Understandably, the Chemical Industries Association is one of the main producers of such information with many detailed and helpful publications on specific substances, a selected list is given on pages 91–2. Other industry-specific publications are "A Guide to Controlling Dust and Fume Hazards in the Rubber Industry", and "A Guide to Reducing Health Hazards in the Plastics Industry" and many others. In this respect it is relevant to mention the Industry Advisory Committees (IACs) which have been described as mini-health and safety commissions for their own industries. They too have produced very useful information for their own industries. Their publications have particular relevance in the sense that they set the patterns for what will be regarded as reasonably practicable for their own industries by others outside those industries, such as enforcing authority inspectors and the courts.

The British Industrial Biological Research Association is also an internationally recognised centre for research in toxicology which produces comprehensive yet concise reviews on the toxicology of selected chemicals. These are called Toxicity Profiles and are available from BIBRA, Information Dept, Woodmansterne Road, Carshalton, Surrey SM5 4DS (tel: 01-643 4411).

Because of the central role of the Health and Safety Executive's annual Guidance Note EH40 "Occupational Exposure Limits", mentioned earlier, it is also very pertinent to refer to the Toxic Substances Bulletin which, also published by the HSE, appears every six months. The Toxic Substances Bulletin acts as a vehicle for the dissemination of interim information between issues of EH40. But, far more than that, it provides news and views on the control of toxic substances generally and gives such information as the programme of work for the Health and Safety Commission's Advisory Committee (ACTS) and its sub-committee WATCH (Working group on the Assessment of Toxic Chemicals).

A list of useful references and addresses can be found on pages 89–92.

Mixtures and synergism

The data discussed so far has been mainly concerned with possible atmospheric contamination by a single substance of interest. However, a complication may arise if more than one substance is used. That is that the combined hazard of the substances can be greater than that of the separate hazards added together. The phenomenon of two substances working together to produce an effect greater than the sum of the individual effects, is known as synergism and has already been referred to. There are probably a number of complex biological mechanisms responsible for many synergistic effects. However, it is also possible for unexpected hazards to arise by the simple chemical reaction of two substances which, in themselves, are relatively innocuous. A comprehensive list of such effects is outside the scope of this book but examples of important possible interactions are presented below. (More information can be obtained from publications such as "Dangerous Properties of Industrial Materials" and "Handbook of Reactive Chemical Hazards".)

Acids + Cyanides = Hydrogen cyanide
Acids + Hypochlorites = Chlorine
Acids + Nitrates = Nitrous fumes
Acids + Sulphides = Hydrogen sulphide
Hydrochloric acid and hypochlorites + Formaldehyde = bis Chloromethyl ether
Sulphuric acid + Methane = Dimethyl sulphate
Sulphuric acid + Nitrates = Nitrogen dioxide
Nitric acid + Copper, brass, heavy metals = Nitrous fumes
Reducing agents or caustic alkalis + Phosphorous = Phosphine

Occupational ill health

It has long been established that occupational activities can cause illness. In the seventeenth century Bernardino Ramazzini advised that doctors in Italy should determine the occupations of their patients. The difficulty with using signs of illness as the starting point for monitoring the environment is that all of the early symptoms of exposure to chemicals (which might include headaches, coughing, nausea and skin rashes) can also have non-occupational causes. More seriously, the onset of physical symptoms in workers may come at a point at which irreversible damage has already been done.

Nevertheless, complaints of medical problems from employees clearly do require investigation and, in two cases, might be cause for particular suspicion of occupational exposure. Firstly, if the same problem is being experienced by a number of employees who work in the same area. Secondly, if the symptom suffered is known to be associated with substances or conditions in the workplace. In any case, this is a problem in which to involve a doctor — occupational safety may involve embracing many disciplines, but they do not include medicine. However, an exchange of information is vital. It is absolutely essential that patients understand the importance of telling the doctor the nature of their jobs, if relevant. Equally doctors must advise employers if they have reason to believe that the workplace may be the cause of any illness.

One particular issue that employers must face is the possible need to set up routine health surveillance to look for illness attributable to work conditions. This is a specific area which is part of the COSHH framework (regulation 11).

In some circumstances such as chromium plating, this is a statutory requirement, but more often the employer must make an assessment of the level of surveillance appropriate to his or her establishment. In Health and Safety Guidance Note MS18 "Health Surveillance by routine procedures", on the subject suggests a graded approach for surveillance, depending upon the seriousness of the hazard. This could range from basic checks which workers could possibly undertake themselves (eg: for skin warts), to higher level screening requiring tests (eg: for lung function) which must be undertaken by specially trained personnel.

In all cases, accurate and clear record keeping is essential. Where large quantities of data are obtained, there is now a strong case for a computerised record system.

Observations in the workplace

We have now considered the possibility that either written information, or reactions by employees could indicate the need for detailed measurement of airborne contaminants. Before presenting the actual measurement techniques it is worth noting that there may also be direct evidence of such contaminants.

Dust

The most common example is that of dust accumulating on surfaces. Clearly such dust must have been airborne at some time and may suggest a failure of dust collection or control systems. This is not intended to suggest that the presence of surface dust is always cause for alarm — it may not be hazardous and it may not result from excessive atmospheric levels. However, the source of accumulated dust is always worth investigating, particularly if there has been a recent sudden change. In any event, as readers will know, there already exist statutory workplace regimes of daily and weekly cleaning to cope with accumulations of dirt and refuse. Those undertaking such activities should be trained and instructed to report unusual accumulations so that an investigation can take place.

Visible indications

Whilst dust can often be observed when it collects on a surface, it cannot normally be seen in the air. The exception to this is when the atmosphere is illuminated by a shaft of strong sunlight. The Irish scientist and engineer John Tyndall used this effect as a practical tool by shining a beam of light from a lamp to observe the movement of dust particles. Although not a measurement technique, the Tyndall beam is an extremely useful way of observing dust patterns, checking the effectiveness of extraction systems, checking ductwork for leaks and pinpointing their exact source.

Use of the Tyndall beam requires a powerful light with a parallel beam (similar to a car spotlight). The light is set up to shine on the area of interest and the observer stands on the other side of the area but slightly to one side of the beam of light. The glare of the lamp should be blocked by positioning a screen between the lamp and the observer without, of course, obstructing the view of the dust.

Direct observation of dust is possible because of its particulate nature. Similar observation of gases and vapours is not feasible unless the substance happens to be a coloured chemical such as chlorine. Even then, visual observation would do no more than identify a leak since the colour will certainly not be noticeable when the chemical becomes dispersed in the atmosphere.

Threshold of smell

A more likely indicator of the presence of non-particulate contaminants is smell. As evidence of hazard, smell has severe limitations because the sense of smell differs from person to person and in any case many highly toxic substances are completely odourless. However, if the substance does have a distinctive (preferably unpleasant) smell *and* if the concentration at which it can be smelt is lower than the concentration at which it is hazardous, then the substance has a useful built-in safety factor. An example is ammonia, a highly toxic gas which rarely causes accidental poisoning because the odour is so unpleasant before toxic levels are reached. It follows that if the odour threshold is *higher* than the hazardous level, as with benzene for instance, the smell of that substance is a serious sign of contamination and should almost certainly prompt further urgent investigation.

Apart from individual differences in the initial perception of smell, it should be appreciated that everyone's sense of smell quickly becomes dulled with continued exposure to an odour. This may well lead to a dangerously false sense of security as the smeller forms the view that what he or she was smelling is now growing less intense. Also it has been suggested in the past, that some gases, for example carbon monoxide which is odourless, may induce a symptom of drowsiness and well-being.

Sometimes, in what is called stenching, low concentrations of distinctively pungent and unpleasant substances are deliberately added to odourless dangerous ones to proclaim their presence. The addition of DMS (Dimethyl Sulphide) in oxygen (not of course toxic but hazardous from the fire/explosion viewpoint) is a recently publicised example to ensure those exposed to risk are made aware of the possibilities of oxygen enrichment.

Chapter 5

Measuring contaminants

Measurement of contamination, once accepted as necessary following a COSSH preliminary assessment (regulation 6), uses various techniques, each one suited to a particular purpose. Dust filter samples and gas/vapour collection and analysis provide indications of contamination, as do certain instant read-out instruments designed for specific contaminants. Atmospheric measurements (regulation 10) are supplemented by biological monitoring of workers, eg: blood and urine tests for absorbed contaminants. This is part of the COSHH regime of health surveillance (regulation 11, ACOP paragraphs 78-87).

Do you need to measure?

Measurement of contaminants in the atmosphere is a complex subject which already fills many textbooks. This chapter will therefore not attempt to give detailed technical information about the various measurement methods. However, it is important to know of the range of instruments available and to appreciate the benefits and limitations of a measurement exercise.

Too often, the response to an environmental problem is to embark on a detailed programme of precise measurement. This produces a lot of numbers and graphs and leaves the problem completely unchanged. Somehow, in the knowledge that the problem demands a response, measurement becomes a substitute for prevention and control.

Thus, if it is clear for any of the reasons discussed in Chapter 4, that atmospheric contamination is unacceptable, then it may well be desirable to direct the main effort and resource into control measures. For example, if there is obviously fume in the atmosphere because operators are complaining about the smell, and if it is evident that the reason is the disrepair of the extract system, then much the best response is to repair the system quickly. The operators will not accept being told the precise atmospheric concentration of the substance as an alternative.

Measurement then, is appropriate if there is a reason to suspect that there might be a hazard. Under COSHH, of course, this becomes a mandatory statutory requirement. Properly undertaken measurement will establish whether this is the case or not, always provided that you know at what level of contamination a hazard exists. This of course, is precisely the reason for the compilation of the occupational exposure limits which this book deals with.

This may seem a simplification and indeed there are other important reasons for measuring contaminant levels. These include:

    (a)   to assist in selection of the correct protective clothing;
    (b)   to observe the effectiveness of alternative control measures;
    (c)   to assess how contaminant levels vary with time or with different processes;
    (d)   to identify undesirable trends in contaminant levels with

a view to taking action before a hazard arises;

(e) to keep a constant check on whether a control limit or recommended limit is being exceeded.

To summarise, measurement can provide valuable information, but should not be undertaken for its own sake. This can be avoided if the objectives of measurement are clearly defined in advance.

Classification of techniques

It will be easier to comprehend the range of measurement techniques if we start by establishing some basic classifications. It should also be appreciated that the techniques for measuring dusts are different from those for gases, vapours and fumes.

The first classification is between techniques which measure the average concentration of the contaminant over a period of time and those which give the level of contaminant at any particular instant. The level averaged over a period ("or time-weighted average") is important if the level varies throughout the working day but we need to know the average concentration (ie: the steady level which would have given the same dose) to which personnel were exposed. It also gives a figure which can be directly compared with published exposure limits. On the other hand, the time-weighted average smooths out variations in concentration which could be important. If, for example, a contaminant is released into the atmosphere when a particular machine is operated, then instantaneous readings would be required to identify the precise problem. It is frequently the case that both time-weighted average and instantaneous readings during a period, are required to obtain an adequate understanding of atmospheric contamination.

The second classification is between "personal" monitoring equipment and "static" equipment. Personal monitors are simply those which are sufficiently small, light and robust to be attached to an operator. In this way, a true exposure of the operator can be measured without having to make special allowance for his or her position and movements. Static samplers, on the other hand, are too heavy, large, or fragile to be carried around and must be used to monitor the atmosphere at a fixed location in the workplace.

It may also be relevant to note at this point, that atmospheric measurement is often undertaken when hazards other than toxicity are present. It might, therefore, be necessary to use equipment which is flameproof or intrinsically safe. In general, equipment which uses mains or battery electricity is not flameproof in its standard form. However, many samplers, including personal samplers, are supplied in a flameproof version and this should be checked with the supplier.

Dust measurement

Dust measurement is complicated by the fact that we are concerned not only with the composition and concentration of the dust but also with the size of the individual particles. This is because large particles (which, if present, may result in a high atmospheric concentration of the substances) do not penetrate far into the human lung. They are trapped in the nose or throat and therefore are less harmful than smaller particles which continue into the alveoli or deepest recesses of the lungs. Since dust particles are not usually a convenient spherical shape, their size is not easy to measure. This is usually overcome by referring to their "aerodynamic diameter". This is the diameter of a spherical particle which would settle in air at the same speed as the particle being considered. These diameters are measured in micrometres or millionths of a metre. We will be concerned with "respirable" dust which is usually regarded as dust with an aerodynamic diameter of less than 7 micrometres.

The usual method of measuring dust is to use a pump to draw air through a filter. The filter is weighed before and after sampling to determine how much dust was in the air. Provided the rate of air flow is known, together with the duration of the sampling period, the concentration of dust in the air can be calculated easily.

It may be that some analysis of the dust on the filter will be required to identify what contaminants are present. This may be undertaken by dissolving the dust in a solvent for chemical analysis, or by examining the surface of the filter under a microscope. The analysis to be undertaken will determine the selection of the filter. They are made in a variety of materials including paper, glass fibre and various porous plastics. Some are marked with a grid to aid particle counting with a microscope.

This method of measurement can be used for both personal and static sampling. Personal samplers use battery operated pumps with flow rates up to approximately four litres per minute. Static samplers can use more powerful mains operated pumps with flow rates up to 100 litres per minute.

If the air is sampled straight through the filter it will, of course, collect all dust particles including those which are large and non-respirable. It is therefore usual to draw the air through a device which separates respirable and non-respirable particles. These normally utilise the cyclone principle in which the air stream is rotated and the centrifugal force imparted to the dust causes the larger particles to be thrown to the side. Each cyclone is designed for a particular air flow rate and will not separate respirable particles accurately if used at a different flow rate.

It must be emphasised that whilst this measurement technique is straightforward in principle, high standards of instrument and laboratory practice are required to obtain accurate results. It is necessary to pay particular attention to weighing the filter (for which a precision balance is necessary), handling the filter with the dust deposit and calibrating the equipment before use.

Instantaneous dust measurement

It will be clear that the filter technique described above will result in a time-weighted average concentration. In other words, the measurement will be the average concentration of dust during the sampling period and will not reveal localised peaks of concentration.

Instantaneous measurement requires sophisticated instrumentation utilising one of the following techniques:

(a) Measurement of light reflected from dust particles.
(b) Comparison of the vibration frequency of a quartz crystal before and after dust is deposited on it.
(c) Absorption of beta rays by the dust.

The light reflection instruments provide a particle count readout (eg: number of particles per cubic metre of air). The quartz crystal and beta ray devices give a mass concentration (eg: milligrams per cubic metre).

Such instruments are usually expensive and heavy and are therefore static, rather than personal, samplers. However, they can be used to plot a graph of dust variations in an area during a working period and can therefore give extremely important information about likely sources of dust, the effectiveness of control measures, and the distribution of dust in the workplace. It is possible that the accuracy of their readings will not be very important because they are to be used to identify peaks, and relative levels only are necessary. However, if accuracy is required they will need to be calibrated in an atmosphere of known dust concentration. This can be achieved by using the direct reading instrument and a filter sampler simultaneously in a steady atmosphere.

Gases and vapours

Perhaps the simplest approach to measuring gases and vapours is to take a sample of the workplace air in a container and then analyse the contents in the laboratory. Suitable containers range from plastic bags to syringes and evacuated metal or glass tubes. An instantaneous sample can be obtained by filling the container quickly, or a time-weighted average by filling slowly and steadily with, say, a small pump.

The problems with such an approach are, firstly, that the contaminant of concern might be absorbed on the surface of the container and not completely released during the analysis. Secondly, even if the contaminant is fully released, its concentration might be so low that analysis is extremely difficult. Such an approach therefore requires a good understanding of the behaviour of the contaminant of concern and of the sensitivity of available analytical methods.

If the above limitations preclude simple container sampling, then an approach similar to the filtration method for dusts can be considered. However, gases and vapours will not collect on a filter paper and must be drawn through a suitable adsorbent material. The adsorbent most commonly used is activated charcoal. After a suitable sampling period, sufficient of the contaminant will have been adsorbed for analysis in the laboratory. As with filtration sampling of dusts, this method can utilise either personal or static equipment.

It is essential that the adsorbent selected is known to be suitable for the contaminant of interest. Adsorbents are available in sealed tubes and, as well as charcoal, include resin and silica gel. If none of these are satisfactory, it may be possible to produce a solution of the gas or vapour using a "bubbler". This draws the air through a liquid solvent and maximises gas/liquid contact by bubbling air through a porous glass bulb. Bubblers are not as easy to use as personal samplers since they must be kept upright.

A recent development in the use of adsorbents for personal sampling, is the passive sampler. These are tubes or "badges" containing adsorbent. No pump is used to draw air through the adsorbent, instead the rate of adsorption is controlled by the concentration gradient of the chemical in question. The higher the concentration of chemical in the atmosphere, the higher the rate at which it will be collected. After a specified period of time, the adsorbent is sealed and removed for analysis. Passive samplers are cheap and lightweight and are therefore ideal personal devices provided they can detect the substance of concern with the required urgency.

With all sampling techniques, however, the positioning of the sampler can be quite critical. Static samplers will sample the general workshop air but the concentration recorded there may differ significantly from an exposure recorded by a sampler on a worker's lapel and even more from a reading taken by a sampler at a worker's "portal of entry" (ie: very close to the nose or mouth). It is because of such variations that it is stressed once more that readings require skilful interpretation by specialist staff. Furthermore, the personal habits and care exercised by workers affect the amount of contamination that they literally stir up for themselves in their own individual microenvironment. It goes without saying that it is this environment which is the most critical for the maintenance of their health. In such circumstances it is almost as important to concentrate on training and supervision as on mechanical control engineering provisions.

Colorimetric detection tubes

A clever and simple method of gas and vapour analysis is the colorimetric detection tube. This consists of a glass tube containing an adsorbent treated with chemicals.

When air is drawn through the tube the chemicals react with the contaminant in the air and the adsorbent changes colour. The length of adsorbent which changes colour is noted on a scale and is an indication of the concentration of contaminant in the atmosphere.

It is important that the detection tube is selected for the contaminant to be measured since each tube can be used to measure one specific substance only. Tubes are available for measuring approximately 200 substances.

The usual method of drawing air through the tubes is by hand using either a bellows type pump or a large syringe. This is the method when a spot reading is being obtained. It is also possible to use this technique for time-weighted average measurement, in which case special long-term detector tubes must be used and an electric pump employed to draw air through the tube steadily throughout the sampling period.

The limitations of colorimetric tubes are that they do not achieve a high degree of accuracy and that the colour change reaction may be affected by the presence of contaminants other than the one being measured. The instruction literature provided with the tubes gives information about gases which would interfere with the desired result. However, despite the limitations they are an extremely useful method of assessing the presence and approximate level of contamination rapidly. They are often a good starting point before deciding whether more extensive or accurate analysis is required. The equipment is relatively inexpensive and is easy to use.

Other direct reading methods

Many electronic and chemical instruments are available for obtaining immediate, direct readings of gas and vapour levels. Most of these are specific to a particular substance or range of substances, though some can be "tuned" to cover a range of different materials.

One class of instruments is an extension of the colorimetric tube approach. In this case the reagent chemicals are impregnated on a moving band of paper, through which the atmospheric sample is drawn. The colour change on the band of paper is measured electronically and can be converted to a reading of atmospheric contaminant level. Gases such as toluene diisocyanate, formaldehyde and ammonia can be monitored in this way.

Other principles used to produce a response which can be converted to a direct reading of concentration are the electrochemical reaction of the contaminant and the heat emission of the contaminant when it is oxidised on a catalyst. In the case of electrochemical measurement, the effect of one chemical on the output of an electric cell is used to give a direct electrical reading of concentration. Direct reading instruments vary widely in their sensitivity and the extent to which the can measure the chemical of concern in the presence of other substances. The selection of the most appropriate instrument therefore requires knowledge of the probable range of atmospheric contaminants and close consultation with the equipment supplier.

Biological monitoring

In addition to measuring contaminant levels in the atmosphere, it is sometimes possible to determine the levels of the substances (or their effects) in the exposed person. Probably the best known biological test is the alcohol "breathalyser" in which alcohol is measured in the breath of the individual. The measurement technique here is either the colorimetric tube or direct electronic read-out.

The substance (or metabolised products of the substance) might also be measured in blood, hair, tissue, nails and urine. This approach involves routine medical surveillance and can give valuable information about chemical exposure whilst automatically taking into account variations in individual behaviour and sensitivity. An example is the assessment of mercury exposure by routine analysis of urine samples for the level of creatinine. If this level exceeds 200 g/litre, or shows a steadily increasing level, there is a possibility of deteriorating environmental conditions requiring investigation.

If the contaminant cannot be measured by direct sampling and analysis, it may be possible to detect the adverse effect of the substance at an early enough stage to prevent serious deterioration. This could involve medical monitoring of factors such as skin condition and lung function.

Such biological monitoring as is mentioned above is part of the health surveillance requirements included in COSHH (regulation 11).

Chapter 6

Monitoring performance

Once contamination sources are identified and their extent quantified, monitoring of performance is needed to maintain standards at a healthy level. This is envisaged by COSHH (regulation 10) which requires, in every case in which it is requisite for ensuring the maintenance of adequate control of employee's exposure to hazardous substances, that a suitable monitoring procedure is employed (ACOP paragraphs 70-73). To accomplish this, policy and procedural matters involving the statutory Health and Safety Policy Statement; the company organisation, arrangements and responsibilities concerning who does what; and worker participation in committees and via safety representatives, are all necessary. Formal surveys and adequate records of them are also essential features. (See ACOP paragraphs 74-76).

Policies and procedures

Any one of a number of factors my initiate a study of the atmospheric environment as has been stated before. These include complaints from employees, visible signs of contamination and the need to assess compliance with the law. However, once the problem is resolved and the motivation for action removed, there is a danger that new deterioration will go unnoticed and that corrective action will not be taken. To avoid this, it is necessary to have monitoring systems which will identify and correct problems at an early stage. This chapter is concerned with policy and procedural matters designed to keep the subject under review and to react to potential problems with minimum delay. As first written this chapter suggested many of the procedures now embodied in COSHH. Its overall relevance remains unaltered, however, because the implementation of COSHH has to become part of management's day to day activities. Wherever in the text a part of COSHH is relevant an appropriate reference is included.

Policy statement

All but the very smallest organisations are required to produce a written statement of their policy with respect to the health and safety at work of their employees. However, the legislation demanding this (s.2 (3), Health and Safety at Work, etc Act 1974) gives no guidance on the style or content of the policy, except that it should contain details of relevant organisation and arrangements. As a result many policy statements are merely bland endorsements of the importance of health and safety and have been long since filed and forgotten.

This is against both the letter and spirit of the law because, properly used, the policy statement can be an active ingredient in promoting and monitoring safety standards. Indeed the concept of the policy statement, presented in the Robens Report, was introduced to dispel the apathy with which health and safety has so often been associated. How then, can the policy be used to monitor atmospheric contamination? We suggest the following checklist of points, many of which are drawn from the Health and Safety Executive's review of the subject "Effective Policies for Health and Safety".

(a) The policy should draw attention to any systems and procedures which affect the environment. These could include equipment purchase criteria, instructions and training for the control of health hazards (regulation 12), arrangements for medical examination and biological monitoring (regulation 11), arrangements for routine surveys and provision of safety equipment.

(b) The policy should identify the mechanism for ensuring that health and safety are incorporated in new projects (regulation 6 (2) ACOP paragraph 24).

(c) The policy should clearly state individual responsibilities so that there can be no confusion about the allocation of duties.

(d) The review mechanism for atmospheric contamination should be defined. This should, for example, identify those responsible for assessing atmospheric survey results and for deciding an appropriate action within a stated timescale (regulation 10).

(e) The arrangements for giving employee representatives (eg: trade union safety representatives) results of atmospheric tests, should be stated.

(f) The policy and its revision should be actively brought to the attention of all employees (through briefing sessions and induction training, etc) (regulation 12 (2)).

(g) The policy should be formally reviewed, revised and re-issued at a stated frequency.

(h) The policy should be dated and signed by the senior member of the organisation to demonstrate full company commitment.

Organisation

It is difficult to make generalised statements about the organisational structure for monitoring atmospheric contamination, because circumstances differ between organisations according to their size, degree of hazard and management style. However, this is a subject that often presents problems, the questions most often asked being:

(a) Which department should undertake monitoring? In sufficiently large organisations the obvious contenders include the medical, safety, quality control, works engineering and personnel functions.

(b) Who has the authority to take action, such as stopping production and implementing control measures, in response to measurement results?

These questions are perhaps too easy to over simplify from this safe vantage point, detached from internal politics. Nevertheless, it seems reasonable to say that:

(a) It is less important which department carried out monitoring than that it is done competently and without risk of bias. This probably rules out non-technical functions such as personnel. Of the technically skilled departments, there is considerable advantage in being able to interpret results against legal standards, etc, which is likely to favour the safety function. The monitoring should ideally not be the responsibility of the management of the area being monitored so that the results can be seen to be impartial and so that results from one area can be properly compared with those from another.

(b) Whilst the monitoring activity should not be a line management function, the responsibility for action must be. A manager is responsible for all aspects of the health, safety and welfare of staff under him or her and must make the decision on production stoppage, control measurements, etc, taking into account the severity of the risk, the priority of alternative actions, and the financial implications. His or her authority to manage should not be undermined by giving other functions the right to override particular aspects of his or her job. This is not to suggest that a manager should not be entitled to rely strongly upon advice received from health and safety personnel.

Whoever does whatever needs to be done to implement COSHH, the employer has a statutory duty to ensure that the persons concerned (whether or not they are his or her employees) have "the necessary information, instruction and training" (regulation 12 (3)). The issue is one of competence and how to ensure it exists in adequate measure in those undertaking work in connection with COSHH. Part 2 of the Health and Safety Executive guide "COSHH Assessments" is entirely devoted to advice enabling employers to choose wisely. It describes the skills which HSE believes to be necessary and also the formal qualifications, practical experience and training that go with them.

Committees

Committees are not always a good thing. Unless clearly briefed and well run, they run the risk of becoming talking shops, discussing issues which could have been better resolved by simple management actions. Nevertheless, committees are an established part of the health and safety mechanism in many organisations. In some cases, as when two or more trade union safety representatives make a formal request, safety committees are required by law. Where an appropriate committee does exist a review of atmospheric monitoring results is an excellent subject for it (regulation 12 (2) (a) and 12 (2) (b)). As in the consideration of the policy statement, it is possible to build up a checklist for reviewing the effectiveness of the committee and to draw much information from Health and Safety Commission guidance:

(a) The safety committee should operate within agreed objectives and terms of reference. These could include a regular review of the results of air monitoring and consideration of, say, an annual report from the safety adviser on the measures taken to control and protect against atmospheric contamination.

(b) The committee membership should be reasonably small (say ten as an absolute maximum) and should have management representation which gives adequate authority to the committee and ensures the necessary input on company policy.

(c) In considering environmental contamination topics, such individuals as the company doctor, hygienist, chemist, etc should be ex-officio members of the committee.

(d) The committee's recommendations should be freely publicised.

(e) The committee's recommendations should result in speedy decisions by management.

(f) Meeting dates should be arranged in advance and never cancelled unless an alternative date is announced.

Shop floor involvement

The Health and Safety at Work, etc Act 1974 and its associated regulations have ensured that many aspects of good health and safety practice are now also statutory requirements, an influence which will be greatly enhanced by COSHH. This is the case with the involvement of employees in matters affecting their health and safety. Liaison with the shop floor is required primarily through trade union safety representatives who must be consulted (Health and Safety at Work, etc Act 1974, s. 2(6)) and provided with information such as measurement results (Safety Representatives and Safety Committees Regulations, regulation 7(2)).

In the field of atmospheric contamination, the provision of information to employees is particularly important. This is because airborne chemicals do not generally present an obvious hazard and, without information about test results, employees cannot be expected to take appropriate protection and control measures (regulation 12).

It is also the case that without shop floor consultation, managers will generally make false assumptions about priorities for action and the feasibility of control and protection measures. For example, it is not uncommon to see dust extraction measures which require time consuming coupling of extract hoods and hoses, etc delayed. Unless operators are consulted about the feasibility of the operation and the effects its introduction will have on production schedules, they are very likely to ignore the extract installation. Similar considerations apply to personal protection measures. The issue of high efficiency negative pressure respirators may be the theoretical way of resolving a dust problem, but their continuous use in conditions of hot or strenuous work may be quite impossible. Only full co-operation with the shop floor will produce practical solutions. The Grant Report, referred to earlier, dealt in highly critical terms with the ignorance, abuse and misuse associated with respiratory protective equipment in some quarters.

It follows that employees must be involved with and informed about, atmospheric monitoring programmes. The quality of the air they breathe should not be a secret, nor should any published guidelines such as control limits. However, these are not easy concepts to understand and cannot reasonably be presented merely as lists of figures. It follows that briefing sessions, explanatory information and maximum involvement with safety representatives, are essential requirements throughout any programme of monitoring and improving the quality of the atmosphere of the workplace.

Surveys

The practical Chapters of this book have dealt primarily with the methods of determining the composition of the atmosphere at any given time, or over a working period such as a day. However, single measurements of this sort are very unlikely to present a true picture of risks to health because conditions will vary from time to time and from one part of the workplace to another.

A properly planned survey programme will obtain maximum information from the measurements and will indicate adverse trends which might require further study. It will certainly be within the letter and spirit of COSHH (regulation 10).

One essential requirement for a good survey programme is advance planning. This will ensure that the hygienist will not arrive on site when the production operation has shut down, or without some vital component of his or her monitoring equipment. Proper planning ahead will also guarantee that all relevant areas are covered in the survey programme and not overlooked through pressure of work.

The second essential is adequate documentation. This includes not only quantitative measurements of flow rates, weights, etc, but also precise recording of the location of test equipment and the activities which were under way at the time. This is certainly an instance where a photograph is worth a thousand words — provided a camera can be used without upsetting the employees, or breaching security rules.

It is worth bearing in mind that a proper survey can con-sume a considerable amount of time and does not just involve depositing samplers and leaving them alone for several hours. The setting up, observing and recording often takes longer than expected and may well require more than one person.

Records

Often the need for good record keeping is evident only with hindsight. For some reason a query arises about measurements of a particular substance in a particular area several years ago. This leads to a daunting confrontation with a crammed filing cabinet which is sure to contain everything except the record you want. The documents which look as though they should be relevant are without some vital item such as the date or a description of what processes were in operation.

It is essential to recognise that retrieval of information from the records might become extremely important at some time in the future. The information may be needed as evidence to refute allegations made in legal proceedings. New information about the hazards of a substance may require a fresh look at old data. Employees may wish to know details of their exposure at some past period of employment.

The problem with keeping records of air monitoring results is the classic problem of all filing and information systems. It is that you never know what factor will be important when you need to retrieve information. If for example you merely keep the data in chronological order as it is obtained, it will be difficult to pull out all the records relating to a particular department. If, on the other hand, you sort the information into department groups, it could be difficult to find all results relating, say, to a particular substance.

The record system will have to be tailored to the size and complexity of the organisation but will almost certainly need some sort of cross referencing. A simple system, for example, would involve sorting records into files for individual departments and keeping the records in date order within the department files. In addition, card indexes would be kept (each card marked with a record location number) with the data sorted into other relevant groupings — these might include names of exposed personnel and the chemicals monitored.

The essential building block of any such system is the record itself. Hastily written notes of instrument readings are likely to be incomprehensible to another person trying to understand them in a few years' time. It is therefore necessary to keep records on an agreed standard layout, ideally a pre-printed form, which ensures that all relevant information is obtained.

A final word on record systems. The task of storing complicated data and then retrieving it using one or two of its many variables, is ideally suited to a computer. Many standard computer software packages are available which can be used for this sort of requirement and it is often more than adequate to utilise low cost microcomputers which can remain within the control of the department producing the results. If the monitoring activity is at all sizeable, it is well worth investigating computer storage.

For a system of COSHH record keeping allied to further general guidance, reference may be made to Croner's Record Keeping Book for COSHH.

Appendix 1

Substances assigned Maximum Exposure Limits (MELs)
(Based on schedule 1 of The Control of Substances
Hazardous to Health Regulations 1988)

Substance	Long-term exposure limit ppm	Long-term exposure limit mg m^3	Short-term exposure limit ppm	Short-term exposure limit mg m^3
Acrylonitrile	2	4		
Arsenic and compounds		0.2		
Buta-1, 3 diene	10			
2-Butoxyethanol	25	120		
Cadmium and compounds		0.05		
Cadmium oxide fume		0.05		0.05
Cadmium sulphide pigments		0.04		
Carbon disulphide	10	30		
Dichloromethane	100	350		
MbOCA		0.005		
2-Ethoxyethanol	10	37		
2-Ethoxyethyl acetate	10	54		
Ethylene dibromide	1	8		
Ethylene oxide	5	10		
Formaldehyde	2	2.5	2	2.5
Hydrogen cyanide			10	10
Isocyanates		0.02		0.07
Man-made mineral fibre		5		
1-Methoxypropan-2-ol	100	360		
2-methoxyethanol	5	16		
2-Methoxyethyl acetate	5	24		
Rubber process dust		8		
Rubber fume		0.75		
Styrene	100	420	250	1050
1, 1, 1-Trichloroethane	350	1900	450	2450
Trichloroethylene	100	535	150	802
Vinyl chloride	7			
Vinylidene chloride	10	40		
Wood dust (hard wood)		5		

Appendix 2

**Prohibited substances for certain purposes
(Based on schedule 2 of The Control of Substances
Hazardous to Health Regulations 1988)**

2-naphthylamine; benzidine; 4-aminodiphenyl (and their salts and any substance containing them beyond a concentration exceeding 0.1%)	Manufacturing and use for all purposes
Sand or other substances containing free silica	Use as an abrasive for blasting (eg: of castings)
Siliceous materials	Use as a parting material in metal casting
Carbon disulphide	Cold-cure vulcanising in rubber-proofing cloth
Oils other than white oil, or oil of entirely animal or vegetable origin or entirely of mixed animal and vegetable origin	Use for oiling spindles of self-acting mules
Ground or powdered flint or quartz other than natural sand or in paste or slop form	Use in relation to certain pottery processes
Dust or powder of a refractory material containing not less than 80% of silica other than natural sand	
White phosphorous	Use in match manufacture
Hydrogen cyanide	Use in fumigation (with certain exceptions)

Appendix 3

"Substances Hazardous to Health"
Definition as contained in The Control of Substances
Hazardous to Health Regulations 1988, regulation
2(1)

"substances hazardous to health" means any substance
(including any preparation) which is–

(a) a substance which is listed in Part 1A of the approved
list within the meaning of the Classification, Packaging
and Labelling Regulations 1984 and for which the
general indication of nature of risk is specified as very
toxic, toxic, harmful, corrosive or irritant;

(b) a substance for which a Maximum Exposure Limit (MEL)
is specified in schedule 1 or for which the Health and
Safety Commission has approved an Occupational Exposure Standard (OES);

(c) a micro-organism which creates a hazard to the health
of any person;

(d) dust of any kind, when present at a substantial concentration in air;

(e) a substance, not being a substance mentioned in sub-
paragraphs (a) to (d) above, which creates a hazard to
the health of any person which is comparable with the
hazards created by substances mentioned in those sub-
paragraphs.

NOTE: The term substantial concentration in air in relation to
any dust is dealt with in the Approved Code of Practice at
paragraph 2(f) as follows "a substantial concentration of dust
should be taken as a concentration of 10 mg/m^3, 8-hour time-
weighted average, of total inhalable dust or 5 mg/m^3, 8-hour
time-weighted average, respirable dust, where there is no indication of the need for a lower value (see current edition of HSE
Guidance Note EH/40: Occupational Exposure Limits for ex-
planation of "inhalable" and "respirable" dust).

Appendix 4

Toxicity Reviews

TR1   Styrene
TR2   Formaldehyde ·
TR3   Carbon disulphide
TR4   Benzene
TR5   Pentachlorophenol
TR6   Trichloroethylene
TR7   Cadmium and its compounds
TR8   Trimellitic anhydride (TMA), 4, 4 methylenebis chloroaniline (MBOCA), N, Nitrosodiethanolamine (NDELA)
TR9   1, 1, 1 Trichloroethane
TR10   Glycol ethers
TR11   1, 3-Butadiene and related compounds
TR12   Dichloromethane (methylene chloride)
TR14   Review of the toxicity of the esters of Ophthalic acid (phthalate esters)
TR15   Carcinogenic hazard of wood dusts
         Carcinogenicity of crystalline silica
TR16   Inorganic arsenic compounds
TR17   Tetrachloroethylene (tetrachloroethene, perchloroethylene)
TR18   N-Hexane
TR19   Toxicity of nickel and its organic compounds

Appendix 5

Selected HSE Guidance Notes in the Medical and Enviromental Health Series of particular relevance to COSHH

MS8	Isocyanates: medical surveillance
MS9	Byssinosis
MS12	Mercury: medical surveillance
MS15	Welding
MS18	Health surveillance by routine screening
MS20	Pre-employment health screening
EH1	Cadmium – health and safety precautions
EH2	Chromium – health and safety precautions
EH4	Aniline – health and safety precautions
EH5	Trichloroethylene – health and safety precautions
EH6	Chromic acid concentrations in air
EH7	Petroleum based adhesives in building operations
EH8	Arsenic – toxic hazards and precautions
EH9	Spraying of highly flammable liquids
EH11	Arsine – health and safety precautions
EH12	Stibine – health and safety precautions
EH13	Beryllium – health and safety precautions
EH16	Isocyanates: toxic hazards and precautions
EH17	Mercury – health and safety precautions
EH18	Toxic substances: a precautionary policy
EH19	Antimony – health and safety precautions
EH20	Phosphine – health and safety precautions
EH21	Carbon dust – health and safety precautions
EH23	Anthrax: health hazards
EH26	Occupational skin diseases: health and safety precautions
EH27	Acrylonitrile: personal protective equipment
EH31	Control of exposure to polyvinyl chloride dust
EH32	Control of exposure to talc dust
EH34	Benzidine based dyes – health and safety precautions
EH38	Ozone: health hazards and precautionary measures
EH40	Occupational exposure limits
EH42	Monitoring strategies for toxic substances

Appendix 6

Bibliography

1. The COSHH Regulations 1988 (SI 1988 No. 1657) HMSO

2. Control of Substances Hazardous to Health
   Control of Carcinogenic Substances
   Approved Codes of Practice (Ref COP29) HMSO
   Note: The above contains the text of the COSHH Regulations themselves

3. Control of Substances Hazardous to Health in Fumigation Operations
   Approved Code of Practice (Ref COP30) HMSO

4. Control of Vinyl Chloride at Work
   Approved Code of Practice (Ref COP31) HMSO

5. COSHH Assessments
   A step-by-step guide to assessment HMSO

6. Introducing COSHH
   Introducing Assessment
   Hazard and Risk explained

   The three leaflets above are free from HSE
   Area Offices, Enquiry Points at Sheffield
   (Tel: 0742-752539), Bootle (Tel: 051-951 4381),
   and London (Tel: 01-221 0870) or from the Sir
   Robert Jones Workshops (Tel: 051-700 1354)

7. **Health and Safety Executive Guidance Notes**

   EH40/89 Occupational Exposure Limits HMSO
   EH42 Monitoring Strategies for Toxic Substances HMSO
   Note: (a)   The January 1989 revisions of both the above are written with COSHH in mind.

(b) EH40 lists the Maximum Exposure Limits [MELs] and Occupational Exposure Standards [OESs] which will apply when COSHH takes effect.

8. A selection of other HSE Guidance Notes in the Environmental Health (EH) and Medical (MS) series of general relevance to COSHH are:

EH18	Toxic substances: a precautionary policy HMSO
EH26	Occupational Skin Diseases: Health and Safety Precautions HMSO
EH44	Dust in the Workplace: General Principles of Protection HMSO

Note: Other Guidance Notes in the EH series relate to specific hazards. Where the subject matter is relevant the GN should be obtained and studied.

MS4	Organic dust surveys HMSO
MS5	Lung function HMSO
MS18	Health Surveillance by routine procedures HMSO
MS20	Pre-employment health screening HMSO

9. A number of HSE Guidance Booklets concerned with health are as follows:

HS(G)10	Cloakroom Accommodation and Washing Facilities HMSO
HS(G)20	Guidelines for Occupational Health Services HMSO
HS(G)27	Substances for use at work: the provision of information (Recently revised) HMSO
HS(G)37	Introduction to Local Exhaust Ventilation HMSO
HS(R)22	A Guide to the Classification, Packaging and Labelling of Dangerous Substances Regulations 1984 HMSO

10 Authorised and Approved List
    Information approved for the clasification,
    packaging and labelling of dangerous
    substances for supply and conveyance by
    road (Second edition) HMSO

In addition to the HSC/HSE publications listed above the following references will also be found to be useful.

11. Frankel M A word of Warning – The Quality of
   Chemical Suppliers' Health and Safety Information.
   Social Audit Limited, 9 Poland Street, London W1V 3DC

12. Sax NI and Lewis RJ Dangerous Properties of Industrial
   Materials. VNR/Chapman and Hall

13. Clearing the Air: A Guide to Controlling Dust and Fume
   Hazards in the Rubber Industry. Rubber and Plastics
   Research Association, Shawbury, Shropshire SY4 4NR

14. Health at Work – A Guide to Reducing Health Hazards
   in the Plastics Industry. British Plastics Fereration,
   5 Belgrave Square, London SW1X 8PH

15. Bretherick L Handbook of Reactive Chemicals.
   Butterworths

16. Handling Chemicals Safely. Dutch Veiligheidsinstituut,
   available from Chemical Industries Association Ltd,
   Kings Buildings, Smith Square, London SW1P 3JJ

17. NIOSH/OSHA Pocket Guide to Chemical Hazards.
   US Government publication available through
   Microinfo Limited, PO Box 3, Newman Lane, Alton,
   Hants GU34 2PC

18. Allergy to Chemicals at Work

19. Chemical Protective Clothing

20. Exposure to Gases and Vapours – Notes

21. Guide to the Evaluation and Control of Toxic Substances in the Work Environment

22. Guidelines for Safe Warehousing

23. Protection of the Eyes

Titles 18 – 23 are available from the Chemical Industries Association at the address given under reference 16.

Index